A Blueprint
for
Corporate
Governance

A Blueprint for Corporate Governance

Strategy, Accountability, and the Preservation of Shareholder Value

Fred R. Kaen

AMACOM
American Management Association
New York • Atlanta • Brussels • Buenos Aires • Chicago • London • Mexico City
San Francisco • Shanghai • Tokyo • Toronto • Washington, D. C.

Library of Congress Cataloging-in-Publication Data

Kaen, Fred R.
    A blueprint for corporate governance : strategy, accountability, and the preservation of shareholder value / Fred R. Kaen.
        p.   cm.
    Includes bibliographical references and index.
    ISBN 0-8144-0586-X
    1. Corporate governance.   2. Corporate governance—United States.   I. Title.

    HD2741 .K327   2003
    658.4—dc21   2002014162

Printing number

10   9   8   7   6   5   4   3   2   1

CONTENTS

Chapter 4: Valuation   **57**

Chapter 5: Corporate Governance Issues in
Investment Decisions   **73**

Chapter 6: Corporate Governance Issues and the Financing Decision   89

Chapter 7: Corporate Governance Dividend Issues   105

Chapter 8: Corporate Governance and Managerial Compensation   117

A Blueprint
for
Corporate
Governance

CHAPTER 1

CORPORATE GOVERNANCE: AN OVERVIEW

INTRODUCTION

Corporate governance is about who controls corporations and why. In the United States, the legal "who" is the owners of the corporation's common stock—the shareholders. However, the reality—even the legal reality—is much more complicated, and the "why" is to be found in historic American concerns about the connections between owner-

1

ship, social responsibility, economic progress, and the role of markets in fostering a stable pluralistic democracy.

Initially, these concerns were focused on the role and responsibilities of the owners of business firms because the owners managed the firms themselves. However, with the emergence of large corporations, perhaps symbolized by the Standard Oil Trust in the late nineteenth century, Americans focused their attention on a new group of individuals: professional managers. Prior to the emergence of these corporations, managers and owners had been the same people, but now things were changing. Now wealthy and often absentee owners were hiring managers to run large, powerful companies, leading to a new set of questions. Among them were: Who were the managers to represent and why? What were the managers' connections to the owners, and what, if any, were the social responsibilities of the managers and owners? Could the managers be trusted to carry out whatever economic and social objectives were entrusted to them? How could they be held accountable for their actions? And, how could they be controlled? In short, what was this beast that came to be called the modern corporation, who should control it, and how should it be controlled?

THE MODERN CORPORATION

The modern corporation, a term coined by Adolf Berle and Gardiner Means, is a limited liability company (limited liability means that the owners are not personally liable for the debts or any other legal obligations of the firm) in which management is separated from ownership and corporate control falls into the hands of the managers.[1] This separation of ownership from management and the resulting loss of direct owner involvement in the firm forced many people to rethink the conventional wisdom about the role of markets and the need for private ownership of capital in shaping the citizens' sense of civic responsibility, preserving liberty, and ensuring economic progress. To explain why this occurred, we need to consider briefly two dominant historical theories about the importance of property ownership and markets for ensuring that Americans would live in a free society that promised equality and fairness for all: civic republicanism and nineteenth-century liberalism.[2]

CIVIC REPUBLICANISM

The term *civic republicans* describes those who believed that a strong link existed between property ownership and socially responsible civic behavior. As American thought and mythology evolved in the eighteenth and nineteenth centuries, many individuals regarded the ownership of property (land, tools of production, machinery, and so forth) as essential for motivating individuals to participate in the political process so as to protect their property from the opportunistic behavior of others. Essentially, widespread property ownership was seen as a means of promoting social and political stability by providing a defense against demagogic attempts to gain control of the political apparatus. Property ownership was deemed necessary for changing human behavior by giving people a stake in society.

Because of this important link between property ownership and responsible civic behavior, property ownership became the basis for the political franchise. Furthermore, citizens' rights and obligations, including commitments to the community and relationships to neighbors, were defined in terms of property ownership. Finally, participation in politics at the local level was considered to be training for eventual civic participation at higher levels—county, state, and federal.

Civic republicans also saw widespread property ownership as a means for achieving liberty and equality. Liberty
meant freedom from tyrants and oligarchs. It meant substi-
tuting the rule of law and the freedom of self-determination—
especially economic self-determination—for dependence on a
ruling class and its benevolent largess. Economic self-
determination, in particular, meant no longer having to
rely on an aristocracy for one's living or being forced to
"sell" one's labor or services to a landed gentry. Instead,
one could get the highest price for one's labor and production in the "market." In other words, it was the market
that made possible the escape from dependency, and so the
market was as essential as property ownership for enabling
individuals to enjoy the benefits of "life, liberty, and the
pursuit of happiness."

Markets facilitated economic freedom by making it possible for people to secure the just rewards of their labor—
rewards that, in turn, enabled them to become economically
self-sufficient. Markets also enhanced economic efficiency by
allocating resources through an arms-length process in
which social status and class were not particularly important
in determining who had claims on economic wealth, thereby
supporting the ideals of equity and fairness. Markets, in fact,
were class levelers that made the objective of economic
equality attainable. So, property ownership and markets were
inexorably tied to each other as the means for supporting
democracy, liberty, freedom, and socially responsible behavior.

But for all this to happen, property ownership had to become and remain widespread. And, equally important, the
markets themselves had to operate efficiently and not be subject to manipulation—the need for transparency in market
transactions was recognized quite early.

LIBERALISM

Those who held contrasting views to those of civic republicans were called liberals. These nineteenth-century liberals, although they also wanted to foster democracy, freedom, and liberty, were more cynical about human nature than the civic republicans. The liberals, unlike the civic republicans, did not believe that you could change human nature through the marketplace and widespread ownership of property. Individuals would be opportunistic and self-seeking regardless of whether they owned property, and property ownership in and of itself would not motivate individuals to become virtuous, socially responsible citizens. Instead, the liberals emphasized the creation of institutional structures, procedures, and governance systems that would fragment or at least discourage the concentration of economic and political power and that would prevent a particular interest group from dominating and taking advantage of other groups. In other words, in sharp contrast to the civic republicans, the liberals did not want to eliminate self-seeking opportunistic behavior—they saw that as an impossible dream. Instead, they wanted to harness it and use it to control peoples' behavior.

But, if the market and property ownership were not needed for changing human behavior (as the civic republicans believed them to be), why were they needed? Well, the market was needed to facilitate economic transactions; barter was not an efficient alternative. And, property was to be used to create economic wealth and generate economic growth. Economic growth was important because if everyone experienced substantial improvements in their economic situations, the problems associated with the unequal distribution of wealth would largely disappear—the old notion of a rising tide lifting all boats.

For the liberals, then, an efficient market and property ownership remained very important. But, for them, markets and property ownership were the means to an end rather than the end in itself, as they were for the civic republicans. For the liberals, the end was economic growth, not a change in human nature.

THE CORPORATION COMPLICATES
THE WORLD

The emergence of the corporation in the latter half of the nineteenth century and the rapid growth of corporations near the end of the century created dilemmas for both the civic republicans and the liberals. For the civic republicans, the goal of widespread ownership of property increasingly seemed unattainable as these "monster" firms grew and wealth became increasingly concentrated in the hands of the few. And without widespread property ownership, human nature could not be changed and people would not develop into responsible citizens.

It is critical to remember that for the civic republicans, economic efficiency was not the ultimate measure by which the corporation—or, for that matter, any other organizational form—was judged. The ultimate measure was whether the corporation supported the development of democratic ideals, freedom, and liberty—not whether it maximized the economic wealth of its owners or any other stakeholders. Concentration of property ownership hindered or precluded individuals' civic development and the maintenance of a democratic society and could lead to a class-dominated society like those in Europe.

The liberals found themselves in an equally precarious position. To justify their political positions, they had to demonstrate that a concentration of corporate power would not lead to class warfare and would not destroy competition in the market and, consequently, the efficiency of markets for allocating resources and supporting economic growth.

In fact, class warfare was already happening. Political coalitions of farmers, small businessmen, and workers had formed and were demanding various reforms. Some of these groups called for a redistribution of property and power. This redistribution was to be brought about by limiting firms' size through such means as antitrust legislation. (Again, note that the focus of attack was on size, not on any question of whether size compromised economic efficiency.) Others made a direct attack on private property itself. This attack sought to enhance the state's direct power over industrial production and appealed to progressive reformers ranging from businessmen who sought to rationalize competition through public or quasi-public agencies to socialists like the early Walter Lippman.[3] Lippman and others like him thought the "science of management" could just as well be entrusted to publicly controlled managers as to private officials. This second attack effectively dismissed the need for private ownership of firms and, hence, private ownership of property. Private ownership, in this scheme of things, played no positive role in supporting economic efficiency.

But who was to control the "scientific" managers? The answer was a democratic political process. The public would limit corporate power through the electoral process, and the whole process would be overseen by a professional civil service. Unfortunately, evidence began accumulating that the political process might have been making things worse, not better. There were never-ending stories of official corruption and of elected officials being bought off by corporate interests. For example, around the turn of the century, Rockefeller interests were effectively in control of a number of state legislatures, and the notion that the political process and public

officials could be used as a check on the concentration of
wealth and as a protection for the ordinary citizen was fast
losing adherents. So, once again, questions about how to
control (read govern) the corporation came to the forefront.
Now, though, attention centered on whether and how managers and insider control groups could serve society's needs
for economic growth rather than simply their own self-
interest.

THE SEPARATION OF MANAGEMENT
AND OWNERSHIP

During the first decades of the twentieth century, people
began to become concerned about two seemingly contradic-
tory developments. The first was what appeared to be a
transformation of American business from family-controlled
firms to firms controlled by a financial plutocracy (financial
capitalism), perhaps best characterized by the House of Mor-
gan. These concerns were exemplified by the Pujo committee
hearings in 1912, set up to investigate whether a wealthy few
had gained control of financial markets. The second was an
increased dispersion of public ownership and the decline of
financial capitalism. What both developments had in common was the separation of ownership and management—a
development that boded ill for the notion that property ownership and management had to reside in the same people
(family-owned businesses, for example) in order to produce
socially responsible behavior.

In reality, financial capitalism (bank control of firms) was
on the wane by the 1920s, so the development of dispersed
ownership eventually began to receive most of the attention.
What was happening was that corporations were obtaining
capital from a dispersed investor base. In other words, many

investors owned small amounts of stock, leaving the individual public shareholder in a very weak position with respect to influencing managerial decisions. As a result, managers and insider control groups (holders of large blocks) could run the company in their own interests and not those of the public shareholders or the public itself. This dispersion of ownership also meant that any connection between property ownership and the development of the citizens' (shareholders') civic and social responsibilities had been severed. So, the public policy question became: How could management be held accountable to the public interest, where that interest was defined in terms of fostering economic growth while preserving democratic ideals of equality and freedom?[4]

Two strategies emerged. One cast the managers as trustees for society at large. The other sought to use self-interest and self-seeking behavior to control stakeholders in general and managers in particular. Both approaches required corporate governance structures that could be relied upon to make managers accountable for their "social responsibility" to enhance economic growth and the general economic welfare.

The Trustee Approach

The essence of the trustee approach was that economic efficiency would be ensured by defining managers as legal trustees for the stockholders' property. In this way, managers could be held legally accountable for any dilution, waste, or misuse of the stockholders' property. In the trustee model, the courts would be the arbiters of conflicts of interest among the stakeholders, especially between management and the public shareholders.

By the end of the 1920s, the trustee approach was well established as the dominant paradigm. Managers were recognized as the trustees of the corporate assets and were seen as being legally liable to shareholders with respect to the use of those assets. This trustee approach received reinforcement from—or perhaps spurred—the development of management as a "scientific" profession dedicated to running the company in a technically sound manner while protecting the other stakeholders from the shareholders (owners). An often-identified spokesman for this notion of the manager as paternalistic trustee for society at large is Owen Young, a public utilities attorney and subsequent chairman of General Electric.

The notion went as follows: The managers were, indeed, trustees. But they were trustees for the public, not the owners, and they had a fiduciary responsibility to the public. Therefore, managers had to and would be expected to balance the public's interests with those of the shareholders, creditors, employees, and so on. Explicitly, this view meant that the rights of the shareholders were limited; they were not at the apex of any organizational or governance chart of the corporation. Young, in a speech dedicating the Baker facilities at the Harvard Business School—a school devoted to training professional managers—advocated that business schools emphasize the public trustee role of corporate managers. Managerial opportunism was to be overcome by well-meaning and right-thinking professionals—and by science.

The trustee approach continued to gain adherents as the country and the world moved into the Great Depression. Now, it came to be coupled with plans to administer the economy through industrial trade groups, cartels, and other such devices in order to deal with what many thought were the causes of the Depression: a mature economy, overproduction, and excess capacity in product and labor markets. Professional managers would join forces with professional government administrators to plan and coordinate economic activity. These ideas manifested themselves in Roosevelt's National Recovery Administration (NRA), which oversaw the development of industry codes and plans but was eventually ruled unconstitutional.

With the legal demise of the NRA, Roosevelt set about establishing regulatory commissions and agencies that targeted specific industries and markets. Investment banking was separated from commercial banking through the Glass-Steagall Act, and a system of bank deposit insurance (the Federal Deposit Insurance Corporation, or FDIC) was established, along with limitations on the interest rates banks could pay depositors. The Securities and Exchange Commission (SEC) was established to regulate financial markets. The Wagner Act and the National Labor Relations Act were passed, as was the Investment Company Act of 1940. Generally speaking, these acts tended to increase the ability of managers to consider all stakeholders rather than just the shareholders when making strategic and operating decisions.

With the outbreak of World War II, managers gained further control of corporations. The war effort had to be coordinated, and managers and public administrators did so together.

After World War II, with managers in control, the trustee approach evolved into managerial capitalism, which peaked in the 1970s. Under managerial capitalism, there was virtually no role for shareholders. Therefore, there was no reason for managers to be beholden to shareholder interests, and certainly no reason to give those interests priority over the interests of any other stakeholder of the firm.

The essence of (trustee) managerial capitalism was that the public corporation was able to sustain itself without shareholders; John Kenneth Galbraith's *The New Industrial State* is regarded as a seminal work.[5]

Managerial Capitalism and the Managerial Technocracy

Galbraith (who was head of the Office of Price Control during World War II) claimed that management—or, in his words, "the technocracy"—so dominated public corporations that the market as it was historically understood no longer existed. Instead, one had to talk about an administered or planned economy if one wanted to understand what was happening.

Because Galbraith saw no new stock issues by large firms, he concluded that shareholders had long ceased supplying the public corporation with capital. Financing, instead, was provided by internally generated funds and banks.

Adolf Berle concurred with Galbraith. In the 1967 reissue of his classic work with Gardiner Means, he writes:

> The purchaser of stock does not contribute savings to an enterprise, thus enabling it to increase its plant and operations. He does not take the "risk" on a new or increased economic operation; he merely estimates the chance of the corporation's shares increasing in value. The contribution his purchase makes to anyone other than himself is the maintenance of liquidity for other shareholders who may wish to convert their holdings into cash. Clearly, he cannot and does not intend to contribute managerial or entrepreneurial effort or service.[6]

Thus, the shareholders had become irrelevant with respect to the risk-bearing and financing functions. And, by implication, public financial markets had also become irrelevant. No one used them anymore, at least not the managerial technocrats of the modern corporation in the new industrial state. What was left for the stockholders to do? Control or monitor management to ensure efficient use of resources?

The Galbraith school discarded the monitoring and control roles of shareholders by arguing that it was in the technocracy's own self-interest to promote growth because growth would enhance management control over assets and satisfy the other stakeholders as well. These other stakeholders could be substituted for the stockholders (the owners). Consequently, the public shareholders of public corporations simply did not have any societal role. And the managers?

Well, by the late 1960s, American managers held themselves out as being society's trustees. Managers saw themselves as the caretakers of democracy who held greed at bay and transformed it into "social utility." So, where were the cracks, fault lines, and fissures?

Challenges to managerial capitalism came from a variety of directions. The "left" wanted to know why financial markets and stockholders were kept at all if they no longer performed any social functions. Why not simply abolish them? After all, many on the left argued, the corporation's basic social objective should be job creation, not economic efficiency. The left was also increasingly concerned with what was judged to be increasing social and economic inequalities that weren't being "solved" by the technocracy. Perhaps the time had come for worker control of firms and large-scale income redistribution schemes.[7]

As the 1970s wore on, U.S. economic performance deteriorated. Rising unemployment rates, double-digit inflation, and a general uneasiness about the performance of the American economy resulted in increasing criticism of U.S. corporations and, as the 1980s appeared, calls for imitating the Japanese and German governance systems. The American version of managerial capitalism was transformed into a call for an American version of Japanese industrial policy and German universal banking and for a move away from markets to a relationship-based governance system.[8] But these calls ran headlong into a revitalized version of shareholder supremacy and a market-based contractual theory of corporate governance.

The Contractual Shareholder Model

Recall that the trustee approach evolved out of a concern about the increasing separation of ownership and control of public corporations and how to hold managers accountable for economic growth. In his classic work on this subject, *The Modern Corporation and Private Property*, Adolf Berle proposed two governance structures for confronting the problem. We have already examined the first, the trustee approach, and seen how Berle moved in this direction in his later years. However, in the 1930s, Berle had misgivings about defining managers as trustees because, among other reasons, he questioned the technical competence of the courts to monitor the managers. Perhaps more tellingly, Berle and others asked why judges and other judicial officials would be any less self-seeking and opportunistic than managers. Who would monitor the monitors?

So, Berle offered another alternative—a contractual solution. In this scheme, the corporation was viewed as a nexus of contracts. Corporate managers would negotiate and administer contracts with all the stakeholders of the firm—employees, customers, creditors, suppliers, and shareholders. However, the managers would be writing these contracts as agents for the shareholders and in the interests of the shareholders. Thus, the self-seeking behavior of all stakeholders other than managers would be held in check by managers seeking to maximize the wealth of the owners. Managers who didn't maximize the owners' wealth would be replaced. In essence, this scheme used shareholders as monitors of the managers to make sure that the managers used resources efficiently and did not run the firm for their own benefit. Shareholder wealth maximization was not an end in itself, but a means to the social objective of economic growth. Of course, the question of how public shareholders would monitor managers and replace them if necessary remained.

Here is where transparency, investor protection laws, markets, and the efficient functioning of markets become critical for a contractual approach relying on shareholders to advance the societal objective of economic efficiency and growth. Shareholders need reliable and trustworthy information in order to monitor management. This information must be available to everyone and not subject to insider (managerial and inside control group) manipulation. A primary responsibility of the government, then, is to ensure that information is disclosed to investors and that insiders cannot manipulate markets. In the United States, the SEC, established in the 1930s, along with similar state agencies, serves this regulatory function. Additionally, investor protection laws protect the property rights of public investors.

Shareholders use this information to collectively set stock prices based on expected profitability and risk. Poor management or attempts by managers to use funds to benefit themselves at the expense of shareholders show up as poor stock price performance. However, unless the shareholders have a way of disciplining or removing the existing management, there is little that they can do other than selling the company's stock. What is needed are ways of removing nonperforming or ill-performing managers. One way is through a market for corporate control in which outside owner/management teams can buy control of a company and replace the existing management with themselves. Another way is to vote the existing management out of office by voting in a new board of directors—exercising shareholder rights.

Ultimately, this contractual approach evolved into modern-day financial agency theory, the framework we use in this book for exploring the implications of corporate governance for managers.[9] The key to understanding financial agency theory is to view the firm as a nexus of contracts among individuals in which the explicit and implicit contracts control everyone's self-interest. In particular, financial agency theory is primarily concerned with the contracts that suppliers of capital write with one another and with managers; hence, the focus of financial agency theory is on managerial performance contracts, security indentures, financial reporting, and governance rules for electing and controlling boards of directors.

More generally, financial agency theory describes a governance system in which the size of the firm is prevented from growing beyond what is economically efficient and through which the self-interests of managers and other contractual members of the firm are held in check by the shareholders. The role of the shareholders is to monitor the performance of management in order to ensure that managers are acting in the shareholders' best interests, which are equated with economic efficiency at the societal level. Ultimately, the shareholders and their agents evaluate managerial performance by looking at the present value of the residual claims on the firm—otherwise known as the market value of the firm's common stock, or stock price for short. The managerial objective of shareholder wealth maximization is more than an end in itself; it is the means to the end of efficient resource allocation and economic growth—at least within the context of a financial agency theory of effective corporate governance.

CHAPTER 2

THE GOVERNANCE STRUCTURE OF AMERICAN CORPORATIONS

A SCHEMATIC CONTRACTUAL GOVERNANCE STRUCTURE

Figure 2-1 contains a schematic model of the American corporation. The owners of the corporation, who are placed at the top of the diagram, supply equity (risk) capital

FIGURE 2-1   A CONTRACTING SCHEMATIC OF THE MODERN CORPORATION

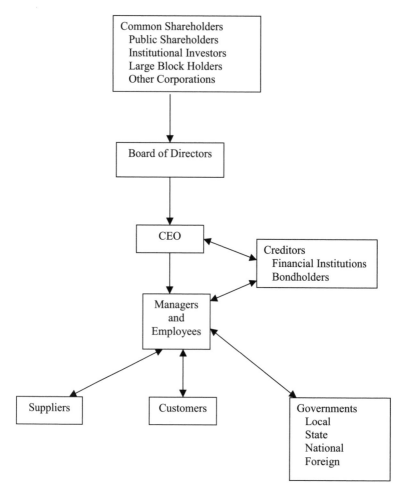

to the company. The contractual nature of equity capital is that it confers property rights to the owners. These rights give the owners control over the acquisition and disposal of the company's assets and claims on whatever assets remain after all other contractual claims on the firm, such as wages, salaries, debt service charges, and taxes, have been paid.

With respect to the company's day-to-day operations,

what is left is called *net income after taxes* from an accounting perspective. Within the accounting model, only two things can be done with net income: It can be returned to the shareholders as cash dividends (or repurchases of common stock, which, as we will see in Chapter 7, is the same thing) or kept in the company, where it remains under the control of the managers. When the net income is kept in the company, it can be used to buy additional assets or to pay off debt obligations.

The owners of the corporation can make their own decisions about acquiring or disposing of assets, running the day-to-day affairs of the company, and what is to be done with any residuals (net income) by themselves, or they can appoint agents to make these decisions for them. These agents, in turn, can appoint other agents. In the Anglo-American governance system, the agents directly selected by the shareholders to represent them are the corporation's board of directors (the board). The owners write contracts (explicit or implicit) with the board, which theoretically acts in the shareholders' best interests. The board then hires a chief executive officer (CEO), who, in turn, hires other managers, and so on down the line to nonmanagement employees. The managers act as agents for the shareholders when they write contracts with the company's suppliers and customers and with other managers and employees. The CEO and other managers also write contracts with those who supply debt financing—financial institutions, bondholders, lessors, and so on. Potential conflicts of interest abound, even within the ownership group itself.

The Owners

Let's start with the owners. The owners are not a homogeneous group; they include: fragmented public shareholders, large private block holders, private and public institutional investors, employees and managers of the firm, and other firms. Figure 2-2 contains information about the owners of publicly traded U.S. corporations from 1990 through 2000.

In 2000, about 38 percent of common stock was owned directly by private households. Except in unusual cases, private individuals do not own large blocks of stock in any one company; more likely, they hold a few hundred shares in many companies—say, a hundred shares in Ford and a hundred shares in Dell. Thus, an individual's percentage ownership in any one company is trivial, meaning that the individual acting alone has no chance whatsoever of influencing management. If you own stock in Dell and you don't like the way Dell's management is running the company, you basically have two choices: sell the stock or wait and hope that something happens that will change the situation.

Figure 2-2   Percentage Ownership Structure of Common Stock of Publicly Traded U.S. Corporations

	1990	1995	1998	1999	2000	Change 1990–2000
Household sector	50.7%	47.9%	43.2%	44.7%	38.3%	−12.4%
State and local governments	0.1%	0.3%	0.7%	0.6%	0.7%	0.6%
Rest of the world	6.9%	6.2%	7.6%	7.8%	10.0%	3.1%
Bank trusts and estates	5.4%	2.6%	2.1%	1.9%	1.8%	−3.6%
Life insurance companies	2.3%	3.7%	4.8%	4.9%	5.5%	3.2%
Other insurance companies	2.3%	1.6%	1.3%	1.1%	1.0%	−1.3%
Private pension funds	17.1%	15.2%	12.3%	11.0%	11.6%	−5.5%
State and local retirement funds	7.6%	9.3%	10.9%	9.8%	11.3%	3.7%
Mutual funds	6.6%	12.1%	16.3%	17.4%	18.8%	12.2%
Other	1.0%	1.1%	0.8%	0.8%	1.0%	0.0%
Total	100.0%	100.0%	100.0%	100.0%	100.0%	
Total in billions of dollars	$3,543	$8,496	$15,428	$19,576	$17,169	

Source: U.S. Census Bureau, *Statistical Abstract of the United States* (Washington, D.C.: U.S. Government Printing Office, 2001).

One possible change agent would be institutional investors. A little over 40 percent of shares in the United States are owned by private and public pension funds and by mutual funds. These are large institutional investors who, through their large holdings, can influence management and effectively threaten management with removal if the best interests of the fund's beneficiaries or owners are ignored.

One of the largest institutional investors in the United States is TIAA-CREF, which owns more than $100 million in each of the largest companies in the country. TIAA-CREF is quite explicit about what it expects from managers: It expects that they will maximize investment returns for TIAA-CREF's participants. Furthermore, TIAA-CREF has developed a corporate assessment program to monitor and evaluate governance practices and policies. Among the policies TIAA-CREF requires are shareholder approval for any actions that alter the fundamental relationship between shareholders and the board, such as anti-takeover measures and the composition of the board of directors itself. Furthermore, TIAA-CREF requires companies to use a "pay for performance" system for executive compensation so as to align the interests of managers with those of TIAA-CREF beneficiaries. When necessary, TIAA-CREF also presses for improved management and operational changes in order to ensure that the investments it makes produce the highest possible returns.[1]

Since 1990, institutional investors have increased their ownership substantially—from 31 percent to 42 percent. Most of the increase represents a shift from direct household ownership of shares to indirect household ownership through mutual funds (household ownership fell by 12.4 percent; mutual fund ownership rose by 12.2 percent). One consequence of this shift from direct to indirect ownership may be that individual public investors actually experienced an increase in their collective ability to influence management through the institutional investors.

The remaining shares of U.S. corporations are held primarily by insurance companies and foreigners. Actually, foreign ownership increased during the 1990s, going from 6.9 percent to 10.0 percent.

Figure 2-3 gives the ownership of corporations in Japan, Germany, France, and the United Kingdom. Note that the ownership structures in Japan, Germany, and France are quite different from those in the United States and Great Britain. In Japan, Germany, and France, private individuals own a relatively small percentage of outstanding stock, especially in Germany, and other companies own a relatively larger portion—more than 50 percent in France. Thus, the dominant shareowners in these countries are other corporations, with the shares being voted by management and not by the public shareholders or by institutional investors repre-

FIGURE 2-3 PERCENT OWNERSHIP OF COMMON STOCK IN SELECTED COUNTRIES, DECEMBER 1995

Ownership Category	Percentage Ownership				
	United States	Japan	Germany	France	Great Britain
Private households	47.9%	22.2%	14.6%	19.4%	29.6%
Companies	1.1	31.2	42.1	58.0	4.1
Governments and public authorities	0.3	0.5	4.3	3.4	0.2
Banks	2.6	13.3	10.3	4.0	2.3
Insurance companies and pension funds	29.8	10.8	12.4	1.9	39.7
Mutual funds and other financial institutions	12.1	11.7	7.6	2.0	10.4
Nonresidents—foreigners	6.2	10.3	8.7	11.2	13.7
Total	100.0%	100.0%	100.0%	100.0%	100.0%

Source: Deutsche Bundesbank, Monatsbericht, January 1997; for the U.S. data, Figure 2-2.

senting public shareholders. These other corporations may have objectives that have more to do with retaining business relationships with the company in which they hold stock and selling goods to or buying them from it than with the public shareholders' objective of share price maximization. Furthermore, the shares of companies owned by other companies are usually voted by the managers of the firm that owns the stock. These managers are more likely to be sensitive and sympathetic to the needs and employment perils facing their managerial peers and to vote with company management rather than with the public shareholders on such major issues as acquisitions, takeovers, and antitakeover proposals.

In Germany and Japan, banks also own sizable amounts of stock in the companies to which they make loans. While these ownership patterns may solve some governance and conflict of interest problems, they create others. For example, do the banks in Germany vote their shares in the best interests of the public shareholders or in the best interests of the banks as creditors of the company?

Ownership conflicts of interests may emerge within as well as across ownership classes. Some owners are in a better position to influence management than others, some owners have more information than others, and some owners may be more concerned about the survival of the firm than others. Holders of large blocks, especially if they have a controlling interest in the firm, can negotiate acquisitions, sales of assets, or even a sale of the company that disadvantages public shareholders with small amounts of stock unless the investors are protected by appropriate security regulations and laws. For example, in some countries, large holders of large blocks can sell their interests to an acquiring company at one price, leaving the small shareholders no alternative but to accept whatever the acquiring company offers to pay them for the now-illiquid stock they own as a minority in the target (acquired) company.

Voting Rights

Some shareholders are also more equal than others when it comes to the voting rights attached to their ownership claims—what are called different classes of common stock. Although this is not especially common in the United States, corporations may issue different classes of common stock, with one class having more voting rights than other classes. For example, Ford Motor Company has two classes of common stock: Class A, with 60 percent of the voting rights, and Class B, with 40 percent of the voting rights. Class A shares are owned by the public, and Class B shares are owned by Ford family interests. Dow Jones, the publisher of the *Wall Street Journal*, also has two classes of stock. Class B shares carry ten votes per share, and Class A shares, only one vote per share.

Governance systems, together with legal protection, security regulations covering the dissemination of information, and insider trading regulations, can be designed to protect the small or public investors' equity positions. Without such protections, small investors are reluctant to buy common stock, and ownership tends to be concentrated in the hands of a few. But, what is the "democratic" solution to the distribution of voting rights, and, how is that related to broader governance objectives concerning how a particular governance structure inhibits or advances democratic pluralism? Should each shareholder have only one vote regardless of the number of shares owned, or should each share carry one vote so that someone who owns 100 shares has not one but a hundred votes?

The early American answer was one vote per owner regardless of the number of shares the individual owned, or at least a limit on the number of votes any one owner could cast—what is called graduated voting. This graduated voting scheme found its way into the charters of the First and Second Bank of the United States and was intended, according to Alexander Hamilton, to prevent a few principal stockholders from monopolizing the power and benefits of the bank for their own benefit. Graduated voting was also common in railroads and manufacturing firms organized in the early and middle years of the nineteenth century. For example, under legislation passed by Virginia, voting in joint stock companies was standardized: A shareholder was given one vote per share for the first 20 shares owned, then one vote for every two shares owned from 21 to 200 shares, one vote for every five shares owned from 201 to 500 shares, and one vote for every ten shares owed above 500. This arrangement lasted until the Civil War.[2]

The Board of Directors

Theoretically, the board of directors is elected by the owners to represent the owners' interests. However, in addition to the problems created by differential voting rights and the composition of the owners themselves, other problems arise. These governance problems include the composition of the board and control over the process for electing the board.

Typically, the board is made up of both inside and outside members. Inside members hold management positions in the company, whereas outside members do not. The outside members are often referred to as independent directors, although this characterization is misleading because some outside members may have direct connections to the company as creditors, suppliers, customers, or professional consultants. These latter may be described as quasi-independent members. The governance issue is: Who do the inside and quasi-independent members represent? Both groups have a vested interest in the survival of the firm and, quite possibly, its growth at the expense of the shareholders. To put it starkly, would the management insiders vote to fire themselves? What about the outside members of the board? Would they vote to fire the managers if new managers were likely to recommend a new slate of directors? In either case, can the shareholders vote any of the directors out of office?

In theory, the answer is yes. However, the proxy (voting) machinery is controlled by the existing board and management. Thus, the control over "voter registration" lists as well as the dissemination of proxy ballots and the counting of ballots rests in the hands of the incumbents, who clearly have a conflict of interest in implementing the voting process.

Corporate Executives and Senior Managers

Below the board in our governance schematic lies the chief executive officer, and below this individual there are other managers, including division managers. We are now inside the organization's bureaucracy, where conflicts of interest abound with respect to allocation of capital, consumption of perquisites, status, and turf wars. Here, the governance task is to control these conflicts and focus competing managers' attention on shareholder concerns. These organizational governance problems extend beyond the managers of the company to its nonmanagerial employees.

Governance-related issues that loom large within the organization are managerial pay and performance and the rules for allocating capital within the firm. Should managers' pay be tied to performance? If so, how should performance be measured? What about allocating capital within the company? How can this allocation be done so that it serves the interests of the shareholders and resolves conflicts of interest among competing management teams within the company? Increasingly, managerial pay and performance evaluation as well as capital allocation schemes are being connected to the company's stock price performance and its cost of capital.

Whether these schemes actually work, though, remains

controversial. The potential problems became very visible with the failure of Enron and other "big name" corporations. Because of these failures, a serious concern has arisen over whether managers "pump up" short-term earnings, legally or illegally (and with the acquiescence of the board and the external auditors), at the expense of the long-run perform-ance of the company in order to collect bonuses tied to high stock prices.

Creditors

We have connected debt financing to the firm through the contracts creditors write with the managers and the board, who are presumably acting as agents for the shareholders in this process. From a legal perspective, the duties and obliga-tions of management, and therefore of the owners, to the creditors are typically spelled out in the loan agreement. Po-tential conflicts of interest between creditors (bondholders) and owners (shareholders) have long been recognized and have been dealt with through positive and negative covenants as well as through the maturity and repayment terms of the debt. Should the firm default on the debt, the creditors effec-tively become the new owners of the company. However, it doesn't always work out this way, and conflicts among credi-tors are just as likely to occur as conflicts among the share-holders.

More recently, debt financing has also come to be viewed as a way of reducing or mitigating conflicts of interest be-tween managers and shareholders. Essentially, debt financing is seen as a way of discouraging managers from growing the firm at the expense of the shareholders and keeping cash in the company rather than distributing it to the shareholders. Interestingly, creditors are likely to approve of managers keeping cash in the company because it improves the credi-tor's financial position.

Relationships with Suppliers and Customers

We have also drawn contracting lines between the managers and the company's suppliers and customers. While it is widely recognized that suppliers and customers are corporate stakeholders, the connections between suppliers and customers, shareholder wealth maximization, and the survival of the firm are not always clear or unambiguous. We think the basic governance problem with respect to these stakeholders (especially suppliers) is how to get them to make investments or other costly commitments that benefit the company but that could be lost if the company engages in opportunistic behavior or fails. For example, an automotive company such as DaimlerChrysler or Nissan would benefit by having its parts suppliers located near its assembly facilities and would also benefit if its parts suppliers invested in product development and technology specifically directed toward Daimler's or Nissan's vehicles. But why would a parts supplier do that if it thought that once the investment was made, Daimler would opportunistically try to recontract so as to lower prices, since having made the investment, the supplier could recover it only by agreeing to these new price and delivery terms? Or, why would a supplier make Daimler-specific investments if it thought Daimler was financially weak and would not be able to honor its contractual obligations?

The Anglo-American governance solution to these relational issues generally emphasizes well-specified contractual terms. Other governance systems, however, such as the Japanese, have historically relied on long-standing relationships between individuals in the respective companies and unwritten expectations of reciprocal actions. Still other arrangements for dealing with this governance-related problem are to have cross ownership between the automotive company and its suppliers so that opportunistic behavior on the part of one party has negative financial consequences for that party. Still another arrangement is to share and exchange managers.

What some observers would describe as convergence of governance systems to a market-based as opposed to a bank- or relationship-based governance system is disrupting implicit supplier, employee, and customer contracts in many countries. For example, Nissan Motor, a Japanese automobile manufacturer, brought in a Frenchman, Carlos Ghosn, to restructure its operations. His plan was to cut 21,000 jobs, close five factories, and scrap half the supplier base to make Nissan competitive in global markets. The plan was described as "another blow to the *keiretsu* system of business relationships [governance structures]. Until recently, these cosy ties . . . helped support a network of friendly companies bound by mutual shareholdings and personal contracts."[3]

AN ORGANIC VERSION OF THE MODERN CORPORATION

When Berle and Means wrote about the separation of management and ownership in the modern corporation, they were concerned with how to make the corporation compatible with democracy in a world in which the managerially controlled corporation had replaced the simple market economy of the nineteenth century. The allure of the pre-modern-corporation era was that it allowed workers to become owner-managers of small firms. This governance structure (ownership arrangement) supported the moral development of individuals and encouraged their active participation in the market and in politics because they had a vested interest in protecting their property from the opportunistic behavior of others. It also motivated owner-managers to act in a socially responsible manner toward their neighbors so as to preserve their property. Consequently, the concerns of Berle and Means and others focused on the societal role of the corporation. They were concerned with reconciling the emergence of the modern corporation with American notions of the moral development of its citizens, democracy, and economic opportunities—what can be loosely described as corporate social responsibility. They were also concerned with how economic efficiency fit into this equation and were seeking ways to reconcile economic efficiency objectives with political and social welfare objectives.

The conflicts of interest that we have identified were important to writers in the Berle and Means era in the context of how to get managers to serve the interests of the community at large and not themselves. The writers were seeking ways to advance the development of character and democracy in America—ways that included enhancing economic efficiency by preventing managers from squandering "society's" economic resources. Who was to say that the only or most desirable way to get economic efficiency was to have managers ultimately serve the interests of shareholders? Shareholder wealth maximization was a means to an end rather than the end itself.

To these writers, corporations existed to serve more fundamental societal interests than making people rich. They existed to provide jobs, develop the citizens' personality, and, if not preserve, at least not hinder the operation of democratic institutions—and, for Berle and other members of Roosevelt's brain trust in the 1930s, to prevent the collapse of capitalism in the face of the Great Depression. For the modern corporation, fostering these societal objectives implied that there were benefits to having the company survive as a social organization—benefits that would be lost if the firm disappeared. From a social welfare perspective, then, corporate governance is ultimately tied to finding ways to ensure that managers do not waste economic resources within the over-riding social responsibility functions of the firm, functions that require the firm to become a organic entity. The ways of doing this and the implications for managers are what we address in this book.

DO MANAGERS ACCEPT THE SHAREHOLDER SUPREMACY MODEL?

One place to look for clues about management's attitudes toward shareholder wealth maximization is a company's annual report and the CEO's report to the shareholders. The H.J. Heinz Company's 1999 annual report is a good example. In a Q & A-style format, Bill Johnson, the president and CEO of Heinz, describes what Heinz shareholders can expect during the 2000 fiscal year. He says: "Be assured that whatever we do will be directed first and foremost towards increasing shareholder value." And he continues with, "Shareholders can also expect continued improvement in return on invested capital, in our use of working capital and in cost reduction. Gross margins should improve further."

Robert G. Schoenberger, the CEO of Unitil Corporation, is also straightforward about the company's objectives. Unitil is an electricity-generating company in a newly deregulated New Hampshire electric industry. Schoenberger, in the company's 1999 annual report, says: "While we can't claim the ability to predict the future [of where deregulation will go], we have set out to be a leader in exploiting changes in our industry for the benefit of our shareholders." He closes his letter to shareholders with, "We are also among a limited few in our industry that are finding new ways to create value for our shareholders."

Georgia-Pacific, in its 2000 Annual Review, described a "brandnew G-P." In this review, management says that

The ultimate measure of our success is the creation of wealth for our shareholders. . . . Georgia-Pacific is transforming our business portfolio to improve investor returns. . . . While total shareholder returns for the 1990s were better than most in the industry, they still fell short of broad equity market returns. . . . This convinced us that something had to change.

This Georgia-Pacific objective takes us to our next topic: stock prices and stock markets.

CHAPTER 3

MARKETS: CAN YOU TRUST THEM?

INTRODUCTION

How do managers know whether they are managing the company in the best interests of the owners? If financial markets are efficient, the answer is simple: Managers should monitor the share price of the company's common stock to find out what public investors think about the company, its future prospects, and its management decisions. And what should managers do to maximize share price? Well, they need to understand how investors value common stock so that they can identify and implement value-maximizing operating and financing policies.

Let's consider the notion of financial market efficiency first—perhaps the most critical requirement for relying on market prices for allocating resources and evaluating management. For if markets are not efficient, the case for a market-based governance system all but disappears. We'll take up the valuation story in the next chapter.

FINANCIAL MARKET EFFICIENCY

Market prices must reflect the true value of a company and its economic prospects if a market-based corporate governance system based on shareholder wealth maximization is to work as intended. But what do we mean by the true value? How do we measure it? And how do we know that the markets (investors) are pricing the company properly?

Financial economists believe that the true value of a company is what investors will pay for that company based on *all* of its expected future returns to its owners. By all, we mean not only today's and tomorrow's returns, but also returns ten, twenty, or fifty years from now. What this definition means for stock prices is that in efficient financial markets, all information about the company that is presently available must be embedded in the price of the company's common stock. Thus, financial markets are deemed efficient if all information about the company is reflected in its stock price, thereby eliminating any opportunities for investors to earn returns greater than a fair risk-adjusted return on investment. In other words, no money trees or free lunches exist. But how do you know whether all the information about the company is embedded in the stock's price and, if it is, that the price reflects the true value? Well, with respect to the information question, financial market efficiency is typically divided into three categories: weak-form or informational efficiency, semistrong-form efficiency, and strong-form efficiency.

Weak-Form Efficiency (Past Prices)

Markets are weak-form (weakly) efficient when knowledge of past price changes does not help in predicting deviations from expected future price changes. Look at Figure 3-1, which is a scatter diagram of weekly percentage price changes for Ford Motor Company's common stock in 1999 plotted against its previous week's percentage price changes. Do you see any patterns? You shouldn't, because the R-squared for the two series—a statistical measure of the amount of the variation in today's price changes that can be explained by having knowledge of yesterday's price changes—is 0.40 percent. In other words, less than 0.4 percent of this week's change in Ford's stock price can be predicted from knowledge of last week's price change; the remaining 99.6 percent is due to other factors.

FIGURE 3-1   SCATTER DIAGRAM OF WEEKLY PERCENTAGE
PRICE CHANGES IN FORD MOTOR COMMON STOCK VERSUS
PREVIOUS WEEK PERCENTAGE PRICE CHANGES DURING 1999

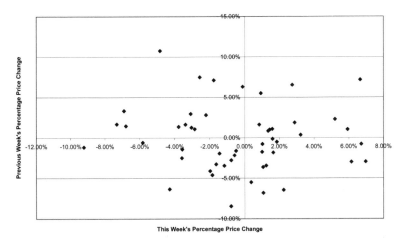

This Week's Percentage Price Change

We conclude from this result that the market for Ford common stock is informationally efficient. The information contained in past price changes cannot be used to predict future price changes; there are no free lunches here!

Figure 3-2 contains a graph of daily closing prices for the NASDAQ index for 2000. To the naked eye, it looks as if a downward trend may have existed throughout 2000, and, a trend line fitted to the data suggests this as well. But before you jump to any conclusions, look at Figure 3-3, which depicts a scatter diagram for the NASDAQ index daily returns (daily price changes) during 2000. Now, this diagram shows no relationship between one day's price change and the previous day's price change—something that you would have expected if a "real" downward trend existed. In fact, if we use the price changes from the previous two days, we still have no predictive value. Price changes for the previous two days explain less than two-tenths of a percent of today's price change—a statistically insignificant relationship.

Does this mean that the level of NASDAQ prices reflected

FIGURE 3-2   DAILY CLOSING PRICES FOR NASDAQ INDEX, 2000

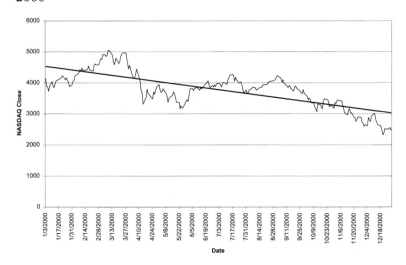

FIGURE 3-3   DAILY NASDAQ RETURNS PLOTTED AGAINST
PREVIOUS DAY'S RETURNS, 2000

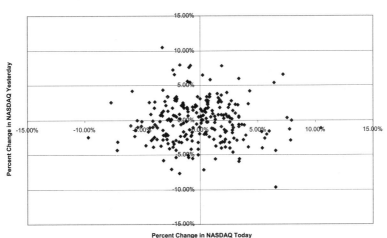

Percent Change in NASDAQ Today

the true fundamental intrinsic value of technology stocks? Does it mean that the NASDAQ was "overvalued" at 5000 in March 2000? No, it means only that the previous day's price changes cannot predict future price changes; the changes cannot tell you whether the stocks are over- or undervalued.

Financial economists and countless numbers of Ph.D. candidates have done all sorts of statistical tests trying to find exceptions to these outcomes. After all, once you found one, you could become rich! But, of course, anyone who did find an exception would not publish it; that person would keep it to him- or herself. Only if it didn't work would you try to sell it to the general public, which should tell you something about how much subscriptions to technical forecasting services are worth. Okay, anomalies do exist; we'll come back to them later.

Semistrong-Form Efficiency (Public Information)

Security prices in semistrong-form-efficient markets incorporate all publicly available information. This information includes news releases about earnings, cash dividends, new product ventures, plant expansions, and so on. In other words, once you've read about the event in the papers, it's too late to make money on the news; it's already in the stock price.

An extensive body of empirical evidence supports the hypothesis of semistrong-form efficiency. Typically, these studies use a technique called event analysis, an analytical procedure that measures what is called a stock's abnormal return around news announcement dates. An abnormal return is a return greater than (positive) or less than (negative) expected given what went on in the stock market that day.

For example, on Wednesday, May 30, 2001, Tyco announced that it would buy C.R. Bard, a maker of health-care products, for $60.00 a share. On Tuesday, May 29, C.R. Bard stock closed at $46.00 a share. On Wednesday, the day of the announcement, the stock closed at $56.09 a share, so the total daily return was 21.93 percent. However, the overall market, as measured by the Standard & Poor's 500 Stock Index, fell by 1.57 percent. Therefore, the abnormal return on C.R. Bard was 23.50 percent, calculated as the actual return on C.R. Bard minus the return on the S&P 500 index, or $21.93\% - (-1.57\%) = 23.50\%$.

We have plotted the abnormal returns for C.R. Bard in Figure 3-4. Observe that, except for the day of the merger announcement, they bounce around zero. But look at the spike for May 30, the day of the merger announcement; it is way outside the band. Also note that the day after the announcement, the abnormal returns fall back to within the normal band and stay there. In other words, no unusual (technically, statistically significant) daily returns precede or follow the announcement-day returns. This pattern is what we would expect in efficient markets.

These daily abnormal returns can be summed together, in which case they are called cumulative abnormal returns. We

FIGURE 3-4 DAILY ABNORMAL PERCENTAGE RETURNS OF
C.R. BARD

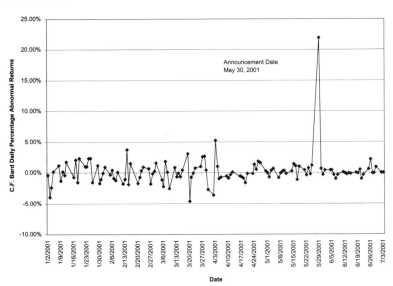

have plotted these for C.F. Bard and for Tyco in Figures 3-5 and 3-6, beginning with January 3, 2001. For example, on January 3, the abnormal return for C.F. Bard was −5.42 percent; on January 4, it was −2.90 percent; and on January 5, 0.21 percent. The cumulative abnormal returns for C.F. Bard, starting from January 3, then are −5.42 percent, −8.32 percent, and −8.11 percent. Subsequent values are calculated by adding that day's abnormal return to the previous day's cumulative abnormal return.

In efficient markets, these cumulative abnormal returns should not exhibit any trend; they should bounce around zero, just as the daily abnormal returns do. Any major price changes due to news, such as a merger announcement, should be incorporated into the stock's price and cumulative abnormal returns on the announcement date, with subsequent cumulative abnormal returns once again not exhibiting any trend.

Figure 3-5   C.R. Bard Cumulative Percentage
Returns Around May 30, 2001 Announcement of
Acquisition by Tyco

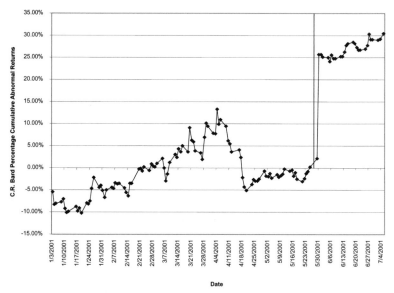

So, what would be some telltale signs of market inefficiencies with respect to stock price reactions to news? Well,
Figures 3-7 and 3-8 contain two examples, one of underreaction and the other of overreaction. In the case of an underreaction, the stock price gradually adjusts to the news; in the
case of an overreaction, the stock price increases (decreases)
by an "excessive" amount and then falls back (rises) to the
"appropriate" value. In both cases, a money tree exists because a trading rule can be used to capture profits. In the
case of underreactions, buy (sell short) immediately on good
(bad) news and watch the stock price adjust. In the case of
overreactions, sell short (buy) on good (bad) news and buy
(sell) after the correction has occurred.

Figure 3-9 contains a plot of cumulative returns prior to
and after announcements of initial dividend payments for
over 200 companies. We can draw two conclusions from this

FIGURE 3-6 TYCO CUMULATIVE DAILY ABNORMAL
RETURNS AROUND C.R. BARD MAY 30, 2001, ACQUISITION
ANNOUNCEMENT

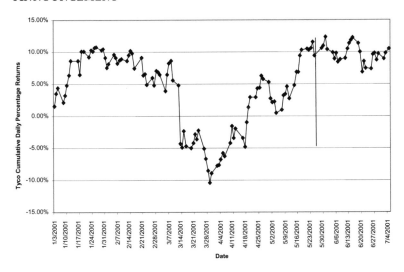

FIGURE 3-7 AN EXAMPLE OF UNDERREACTION TO NEWS ON
DAY 0

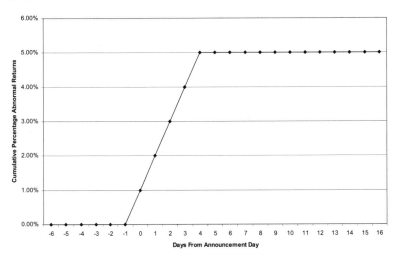

Figure 3-8   An Example of Prices Overreacting to News on Day 0

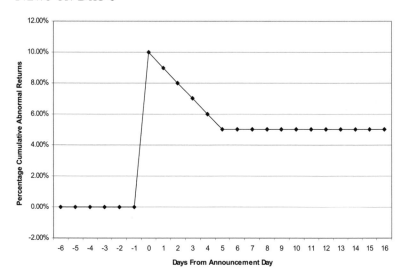

Figure 3-9   Cumulative Abnormal Returns for Initial Dividend Announcements

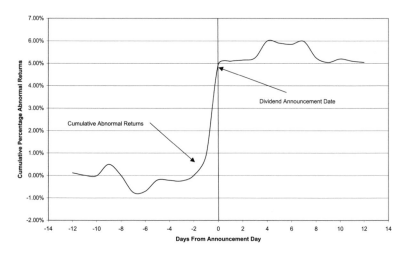

graph: First, initial dividend payments were greeted as good news by investors, and second, investors immediately incorporated the news of the initial dividend payment into stock prices. No rise (or fall) in price persisted in the days following the announcement. No rise in stock prices occurred prior to the announcement. And stock prices did not over- or underreact to the announcement.

The evidence with regard to semistrong-form market efficiency is overwhelming. For all practical purposes, news about financing, investment, dividend, and organizational restructuring decisions (such as mergers and acquisitions) is immediately reflected in market prices. We will use the findings of many of these studies in subsequent chapters to explain the connections between managerial decisions and shareholder wealth maximization.

Strong-Form Efficiency

Strong-form-efficient markets incorporate private as well as public information in security prices. Obviously, managers and other insiders have information that they can trade on before the information becomes public. So, the potential exists for managers to make a small fortune by taking advantage of this informational asymmetry. This poses a serious problem for governance and for regulation of financial markets.

If public investors believe that managers and other insiders will take advantage of their privileged information, these investors will be reluctant to invest in the company or will do so only at a highly discounted price. In effect, if this happens, investors can no longer assume that market prices represent the true value of the company. To prevent such a breakdown in markets, a market-based governance structure requires insider-trading laws to maintain the public's confidence. Therefore, as a manager, you are not permitted to act on inside information. You can try, but it is illegal, and you may end up in jail—especially if you are too greedy about it!

More to the point with regard to the question of whether financial markets are strong-form-efficient is the question of whether professional investors can consistently outperform or "beat" the market. This proposition has been tested by examining whether professional mutual fund managers can outperform randomly constructed stock portfolios or index funds. Time and again, the answer is no.

One of the most widely regarded studies of mutual fund performance was done by Burton Malkiel, who examined the returns from investing in mutual funds between 1971 and 1991. He concluded that

> [his] study of mutual funds does not provide any reason to abandon a belief that securities markets are remarkably efficient. Most investors would be considerably better off by purchasing a low expense index fund, than by trying to select an active fund manager who appears to posses a "hot hand." Since active management generally fails to provide excess returns and tends to generate greater tax burdens for investors, the advantage of passive management holds, a fortiori.[1]

Figure 3-10 provides some less scientific evidence. This figure contains annualized five-year returns for various categories of general stock mutual funds for May 1996 through May 2001. Not a single group of funds was able to outperform the S&P 500 index. And the best-performing fund group was the one that followed the passive investment strategy recommended by Malkiel—that of indexing on the S&P 500.

FIGURE 3-10   5-YEAR ANNUALIZED PERFORMANCE OF
GENERAL STOCK FUNDS VERSUS THE S&P 500 INDEX

Fund Investment Objective	5-Year Annualized Return, %	Fund Return Better/(Worse) than S&P 500 Index, %
Large-cap core funds	12.31	(2.59)
Large-cap growth funds	11.79	(3.11)
Large-cap value funds	12.71	(2.19)
Mid-cap core funds	13.60	(1.30)
Mid-cap growth funds	9.63	(5.27)
Mid-cap value funds	12.68	(2.22)
Small-cap core funds	10.52	(4.38)
Small-cap growth funds	8.20	(6.70)
Small-cap value funds	12.18	(2.72)
S&P 500 index funds	14.39	(0.51)
S&P 500 Index	14.90%	

Source: Lipper, *Wall Street Journal*, June 4, 2001, p. R5

MARKET INEFFICIENCIES AND ANOMALIES

Do market inefficiencies exist? A number of anomalies have been identified and remain largely unexplained. For managers, arguably the two most important anomalies are the price behavior of (1) initial public offerings (IPOs) and (2) earnings announcements.

IPOs

Perhaps because they remain an enigma, IPOs have fascinated financial economists and practitioners for years. Here's why. The typical IPO is underpriced. By underpriced, we mean that the price at which its shares are offered to the public (something of a misnomer because institutions are often the initial buyers) is, on average, about 10 to 12 percent below the first trading price (the first secondary-market transaction price). In the 1990s, this underpricing was even greater, especially among high-tech and Internet IPOs. For example, on August 5, 1995, Netscape went public at an offering price of $28 a share. At the end of trading on the first day, the price was $54—almost double the offering price. In the jargon of finance, the founders of Netscape "left a lot of money on the table." Why wasn't the stock priced much higher?

How about this one? On March 31, 2000, ArrowPoint Communications Inc. went public at $34 a share on the NASDAQ. Late in the afternoon of March 31, the shares traded at $96, for an underpricing of $62 a share! ArrowPoint had about 34.2 million shares outstanding after the IPO, so the company left $2,120,400,000 on the table.

Here's another puzzle: The stock price of the typical IPO does worse than the average stock (underperforms the market) during its first three years of trading. Why? Do investors overprice the stock initially? If so, why don't investors learn from past experiences? We don't know. We just know that both this underperformance and the aforementioned underpricing occur in just about every country.[2]

Earnings Announcements

Publicly owned corporations publish quarterly financial statements that include quarterly earnings. In efficient markets, any earnings "surprises" should be immediately incorporated into the company's stock price. However, the evidence suggests that they are not.

The stock price of a company that announces a very negative earnings surprise (earnings are way below expectations) drifts downward for about ninety days after the announcement of the surprise. The stock price of a company that announces a very positive earnings surprise does just the opposite: The stock price of such a company drifts upward for about ninety days.[3]

Why? We don't know.

The 2000 NASDAQ Crash

On March 10, 2000, the NASDAQ closed at 5048. By the end of the year, the index stood at 2470, for a loss of almost 50 percent. Is this drop consistent with notions of market efficiency? Or is it more consistent with some notion of an irrational speculative bubble and grounds for rejecting any assertions that market prices reflect true intrinsic fundamental values? After all, how can you explain why Cisco could be worth $137 a share on March 10, 2000, and only $38.25 a share at year-end? Well, here the advocates of financial market efficiency draw an important distinction between the absolute level of prices and relative prices.

Suppose investors accepted the proposition that the most recent price of a stock was the best estimate of its intrinsic value. In our example, on March 10, 2000, that would be $137 for Cisco. Then, as news arrived about the company, the most recent price would move up or down accordingly. But what if investors were to collectively decide that $137 was no longer the appropriate benchmark against which to price daily news because they had lost confidence in the prospects for all "new-economy" companies. Now we could have a major price drop or increase as investors revised their notion of what Cisco's absolute price should be. Furthermore, other new-economy companies such as Altera Corporation and Intel Corporation would experience similar price drops. So, where are we?

Well, while we might question whether absolute stock prices are good indicators of intrinsic value, we remain on rather firm ground if we stick with relative price changes. For example, if Cisco's earnings prospects improve substantially relative to those of other new-economy companies, we can be pretty sure that this will result in an increase in Cisco's stock price relative to the prices of the other companies. And, for managers who want to know what investors think about their performance relative to that of their competitors, this is what is critical.

WHAT MARKET EFFICIENCY MEANS FOR MANAGERS AND GOVERNANCE

Arguably, the most important message of market efficiency for managers is that the company's stock price is a reliable measure of whether managers are running the company in the long-run best interests of the shareholders. Also, changes in the stock price provide information about whether managerial investment and financing decisions are value-creating or value-destroying.

How Are We Doing?

For example, on February 21, 2001, Procter & Gamble and Coca-Cola announced a $4.25 billion joint venture to sell juice, juice-based drinks, and snacks. The venture was to be a limited-liability company with 50 percent owned by Procter & Gamble and 50 percent owned by Coca-Cola. Coca-Cola would transfer its entire Minute Maid juice line to the venture, and Procter & Gamble would transfer two brands: Sunny Delight Drinks and Pringles potato chips. Was this a good deal for both companies, a good deal for neither, or good for one and bad for the other? What about in total? To answer these questions, we can look at what happened to the stock prices and market values of these two companies on the announcement day. The data are contained in Figure 3-11.

On the day of the announcement, Procter & Gamble stock rose 1.44 percent, from $75.71 to $76.80 a share. However, the overall market, as measured by the S&P 500 index, fell by 0.98 percent. Thus, after taking the overall market into account, the abnormal return for Procter & Gamble was a positive 2.42 percent. With 1.3 billion shares outstanding, the dollar value of this joint venture to Procter & Gamble shareholders was $2.381 billion. P&G management can conclude that they have made an investment (adopted a strategy) that was good for the owners of P&G.

The same cannot be said for Coca-Cola (Coke). Coke's

FIGURE 3-11 VALUATION EFFECTS OF PROCTER & GAMBLE AND COCA-COLA JOINT VENTURE ANNOUNCEMENT, FEBRUARY 21, 2001

	Procter & Gamble	Coca-Cola	Combined
Stock price February 20	$75.71	$58.42	
Stock price February 21	$76.80	$54.92	
Dollar change	+ $1.09	− $3.50	
Percent change	1.44%	− 5.99%	
Percent change in S&P 500 index	− 0.98%	− 0.98%	
Stock price change adjusted for change in S&P 500 index: abnormal return	+ 2.42%	− 5.01%	
Number of shares	1.300 billion	2.490 billion	
Market value February 20	$98.423 billion	$145.466 billion	$243.889 billion
Market value February 21	$99.840 billion	$136.751 billion	$236.591 billion
Change in market value	+ 1.417 billion	− $8.715 billion	− $7.298 billion
Change in market value adjusted for change in S&P 500 index: abnormal dollar return	**+ 2.381 billion**	**− $7.289 billion**	**− $4.908 billion**

stock price fell 5.99 percent, from $58.42 to $54.92, for a loss in total market value of $8.715 billion. Adjusted for the overall market, the abnormal dollar loss was $7.289 billion. Thus, when Coke's managers looked to see what investors— including institutional investors—thought of their strategy, the answer is, "Not much." Coke's managers destroyed value.

What about the overall value of this proposed joint venture? Did investors think the project would be value-creating or value-destroying on a combined basis? Well, investors didn't like the overall project. The combined market value of both companies, adjusted for the market, fell by $4.908 billion. What this negative value means is that investors believed the project should never have been undertaken.

Interestingly, on July 5, 2001, the two companies jointly announced that they were rethinking the deal. Market analysts ascribed the rethinking to P&G's getting the better of the deal. One analyst even recommended that Coke walk away entirely, while another analyst suggested that Coke start its own juice division.[4]

Don't Try to Outguess or Beat the Market

Corporate managers, especially financial managers, must develop and implement plans for financing the company and managing its financial risks. The financing decisions involve choices about when to raise capital and whether to use debt or equity. The risk management decisions involve choices about whether to hedge exchange-rate, interest-rate, and commodity-price risks.

Let's take the case of a manager who needs to raise $300 million to finance a major expansion program. The manager could sell either bonds or common stock. Should the manager make this decision on the basis of whether the stock has risen or fallen over the past year or whether interest rates are above or below some benchmark level? If financial markets are efficient, the answer to these questions is no. The current stock price is the best estimate of what the company is worth, and, as we showed earlier, past stock prices cannot be used to predict future stock prices. In effect, the manager is assuming that he can beat the market if he conditions the decision about selling stock on whether the stock has moved up or down in the last month, quarter, or year. Think of it this way: If professional mutual fund managers cannot predict what the market will do, why should the manager of a business firm be any more successful?

The same holds true for interest rates. Investors' and borrowers' expectations of interest rates are captured in the yield curve or term structure of interest rates and in the prices of interest-rate financial contracts. The manager, by taking a view on whether interest rates will be lower or higher in the future, is, in effect, trying to outguess the market. Again, the overwhelming evidence is that hardly anyone has been able to do so consistently.

What holds for stock prices and interest rates also holds for foreign exchange rates and commodity prices. Taking a position on exchange rates or commodity prices can be dangerous. The objective should be to stabilize cash flows and protect the firm from exchange-rate and commodity-price volatility through risk management strategies rather than trying to play the foreign exchange markets.

Don't Try to Fool Investors

Managers who believe that investors are myopic and focus only on short-term financial results may try to manipulate earnings through creative accounting techniques—legal, illegal, and otherwise. Such measures include booking transfers of inventory as sales, writing up assets, selective booking of sales and expenses, and keeping debt off the balance sheet.

Don't do it. Eventually, investors will see through legal ways of manipulating earnings. They may miss the illegal ones, but, should these methods come to light, the consequences for the managers could be severe, including criminal prosecution for fraud.

For example, the penalties paid by Enron for using aggressive accounting procedures such as keeping debt off its balance sheet and manipulating earnings have been enormous. The company was forced to file for bankruptcy, and its senior managers have suffered severe damage to their reputations and financial positions and face civil and criminal charges. Enron's auditor, Arthur Andersen, has suffered similar consequences. The firm has lost numerous audit clients and now no longer exists as an independent firm.

Other companies have also paid a price for the Enron-Andersen fiasco. A new term, the "Enron premium," has entered Wall Street's vocabulary. The term refers to the drop in stock prices suffered by many firms as investors began looking around for other Enrons.

Some additional examples of the trouble managers get into when they pursue accounting policies that are aggressive at best include the following:[5]

❐ An ex-vice chairman of Coca-Cola pleaded guilty in September 2001 to concealing expenses at Aurora Foods.

❐ A past CFO of Lesley Fay was sentenced in February 2002 to nine years in prison for a variety of sales-padding ploys.

❐ Two managers of Sirena Apparel pleaded guilty to revenue-inflating schemes.

❐ David Thatcher, president of Critical Path, Incorporated, pleaded guilty to faking or backdating sales to meet quarterly revenue targets.

We'll have more to say about possible connections between these attempts to inflate earnings and stock prices
when we consider management compensation schemes.

TRANSPARENCY AND MARKET EFFICIENCY

We cannot emphasize enough that if markets are to be efficient, investors must receive trustworthy financial information about companies. The public policy question is how to
ensure that this happens.

In the United States, the financial reporting rules that
companies must follow are established by a privately funded
group called the Financial Accounting Standards Board, better known as FASB. Who funds FASB? The major accounting
firms that audit the financial statements of publicly held corporations. Well, so far so good. But, what happens when the
major accounting firms that fund and control FASB begin to
do consulting for the same firms whose books they audit?
And what happens when the auditors are effectively chosen
by the management of the audited companies rather than
by the shareholders (who, in theory, are doing the selecting
through the board of directors)?

Well, at least two bad things can happen. One is that the
accounting rules will be promulgated in such a way that they
work to the advantage of the firms being audited, thereby
encouraging the aggressive accounting that has become associated with Enron, Global Crossing, Tyco, Boston Chicken,
and other firms that are now in the public limelight. The
other is that the auditors, as they make more and more
money from selling consulting services to their auditing clients, will conspire with management to make the company
look good, or at least look the other way while the company

engages in questionable financial reporting practices. Both outcomes are bad for public investors and bad for financial markets.

How important is the consulting business to the firms that audit the books of major corporations? Based on recent SEC filings (see Figure 3-12), almost every company in the Dow Jones Industrial Average paid its auditors more for consulting and other services than for auditing the books. Since 1970, auditing fees for the big accounting firms have fallen from 70 percent of total revenue to about 34 percent. Furthermore, the accounting firm partners who bring in the consulting fees are more highly paid than those that do just the auditing, thereby exacerbating an already potentially destructive conflict of interest between the auditor's role of verifying the financial statements for the public shareholders and the profits of the firms that do the auditing.

What is the solution? The following have been proposed:

- ❏ Prohibit auditors from also selling consulting services to their clients. Either be an auditor or a consultant.
- ❏ Have a government agency take over the role of FASB and set the accounting standards.
- ❏ Require corporations to change auditors every three or five years.
- ❏ Require the CEO and the board of directors to personally certify the integrity of the financial statements.
- ❏ Hold the CEO and the board of directors criminally liable if the company fails to comply with accounting rules and/or issues false or misleading information.

FIGURE 3-12   AUDIT AND NONAUDIT FEES PAID BY THE
COMPANIES IN THE DOW JONES INDUSTRIAL AVERAGE 2000
AND 2001 PROXY STATEMENTS

Company	Audit Fees (millions of $)	Other Fees (millions of $)	Other Fees as a Percentage of Total Fees
SBC Communications	$3.0	$35.3	92.17%
International Paper	4.7	30.7	86.72%
AT&T	7.9	48.4	85.97%
Honeywell	5.1	27.8	84.50%
Walt Disney	8.7	43.0	83.17%
Coca-Cola	5.0	23.9	82.70%
General Motors	17.0	79.0	82.29%
Johnson & Johnson	9.3	43.1	82.25%
DuPont	7.0	30.0	81.08%
IBM	12.2	51.0	80.70%
J. P. Morgan Chase	21.3	84.2	79.81%
ExxonMobil	18.3	65.3	78.11%
Home Depot	1.0	3.5	77.78%
American Express	7.4	25.0	77.16%
Caterpillar	7.6	25.6	77.11%
General Electric	23.9	79.7	76.93%
Microsoft	4.7	14.7	75.77%
Eastman Kodak	3.8	10.8	73.97%
United Technologies	9.1	25.8	73.93%
Boeing	10.5	24.3	69.83%
McDonald's	2.7	6.2	69.66%
Phillip Morris	17.3	29.3	62.88%
3M	4.5	7.2	61.54%
Intel	4.1	5.9	59.00%
Procter & Gamble	11.0	15.8	58.96%
Alcoa	5.7	6.9	54.76%
Citigroup	26.1	24.6	48.52%
Wal-Mart Stores	2.8	2.0	41.67%
Merck	4.2	2.1	33.33%

Source: SEC filings reported in "Accounting Industry Fights Calls for 'Audit Only' Rules," *Wall Street Journal,* March 7, 2002, p. C1.

CHAPTER 4

VALUATION

INTRODUCTION

I f you are willing to accept the idea that financial markets are efficient, the next question becomes one of how investors price common stocks. What do they consider important? What do they consider irrelevant? And how do they decide what is the required rate of return for their money?

VALUING COMMON STOCK

The basic stock price valuation model is a discounted cash flow model in which the stock price is modeled as the present (discounted) value of the cash flows the investor expects to receive from owning the share. The model is often called the dividend valuation model because it can be represented mathematically as

$$P_0 = \sum_{t=1}^{\infty} \frac{D_t}{(1+k)^t}$$

where
P_0 = the price per share today
D_t = the expected per share cash dividend at the end of year t
k = the investors' risk-adjusted required rate of return on the stock

And, if per share cash dividends are expected to grow by a constant annual percentage rate g forever and ever, the model reduces to

$$P_0 = \frac{D_1}{k-g}$$

The discount rate used is the investors' risk-adjusted required rate of return k, which is the return an investor can earn on other financial assets of identical risk. The manager should think of this required rate of return as the risk-adjusted return that the company must earn on investments in real assets.

For example, suppose the expected per share cash dividend for Ford Motor Company next year, D_1, is $1.30; the investors' required rate of return k on Ford's common stock is 9.00 percent; and investors expect the annual growth rate g for Ford's per share cash dividends to be 5.00 percent. With these expectations, we would estimate Ford's stock price today to be $32.50 a share. The actual stock price may be more or less than $32.50, in which case, if you believe that markets are efficient, you have erred in estimating the dividend, the required rate of return, or the expected dividend growth rate.

As you can observe from the model, increases (decreases) in expected cash dividends and dividend growth rates cause an increase (decrease) in the stock price, as does a decrease (increase) in the investors' required rate of return. Now we know how Ford managers can increase shareholder wealth: They can adopt policies that, other things being equal, lead to increases in cash dividends (either today or in the distant future) and/or lower the investors' required rate of return. Let's start with cash dividends.

Cash Dividends and Earnings

Cash dividends are paid out of earnings generated by investments in physical and human capital—let's call it tangible and intangible capital. The higher the earnings, the higher the potential cash dividends. Thus, managers can increase shareholder wealth by making investments (in products, technologies, and so on) that generate high earnings, either today or in the future. Of course, these investments themselves require cash, so managers frequently have to choose between distributing the company's earnings today as dividends or reinvesting them in the company to generate even higher earnings and cash flows in the future. It is this reinvestment of earnings in high-return projects today that produces an increase in *g*, the expected annual growth rate in cash dividends.

Investors' Required Rate of Return

Knowledge about what determines the investors' required rate of return is critical for managers who want to maximize the company's stock price and for managers whose performance evaluation and compensation are tied to the market value of the company. So, let's begin by breaking the investors' required rate of return into two components: the risk-free nominal interest rate (RF) and a risk premium (RP). The risk-free nominal interest rate is the interest rate on default-free U.S. government bonds. Managers have no control over this rate; it is the same for every company. The risk premium depends on the riskiness of the firm's after-tax cash flows to shareholders. Managers have varying degrees of control over this component.

Although most financial economists and practitioners believe that investors require higher rates of return as the riskiness of the investment increases, disagreement exists about just what risks investors are concerned about and how these risks are incorporated into stock prices. Basically, the issue boils down to whether investors factor into the price the total risk of a stock or only that portion of the risk that cannot be eliminated by holding the stock as part of a diversified investment portfolio.

Figure 4-1 contains information about the historical returns that investors have earned on a variety of common

Figure 4-1   Average Annual Returns, Risk Premiums, and Standard Deviation of Returns for Selected Security Portfolios, 1926–1998

Portfolio	Average Annual Return	Risk Premium Versus Long-Term U.S. Government Bonds	Standard Deviation of Annual Returns
Large-company stocks	13.2%	7.5%	20.3%
Small-company stocks	17.4%	11.7%	33.8%
Long-term corporate bonds	6.1%	0.4%	8.6%
Long-term U.S. government bonds	5.7%	—	9.2%

Source: Ibbotson Associates: Stocks, Bonds, Bills, and Inflation 1999 Yearbook (Chicago: Ibbotson Associates, Inc.).

stock portfolios and the riskiness of these portfolios. Since 1926, the yearly return that investors have earned on a portfolio of large-company stocks (such as the *Fortune* 500 companies) has averaged 13.2 percent. The yearly average for a portfolio of small-company stocks has been 17.4 percent. The average default-risk-free nominal rate of return on long-term U.S. government bonds has been 5.7 percent. So, at least in the United States, investors were able to earn considerably more on common stock investments than on risk-free bonds. However, the returns on common stocks were also considerably more risky. Risk, as measured by the yearly standard deviation of annual returns, was 33.2 percent for the small-stock portfolio, 20.3 percent for the large-company portfolio, and 5.7 percent for the default-free government bonds. In other words, for investors to reach for the higher average returns on small stocks, they had to accept a much greater variation in year-to-year returns than on government bonds.

If we look at the standard deviation of the typical single stock and not a portfolio of stocks, however, it is around 50 percent even though the average expected return is the same as the portfolio return. Why? Well, the answer is that much of the risk associated with a single stock can be eliminated through diversification—holding the stocks of many different companies. The risk that can be eliminated through diversification is called *unique risk* and includes such risks as the success of the company's advertising programs, new product developments, and changes in the company's competitive position within its industry. The risk that cannot be eliminated is called *market risk*. Market risk refers to the effects that events that affect all companies in a country, such as interest-rate changes, recessions, and economic expansions, have on the financial fortunes of the company.

So, which risk should managers focus on when they evaluate the likely outcome of specific investment and financing decisions on the company's stock price? Total risk or market risk?

THE CAPITAL ASSET PRICING MODEL

A commonly used asset pricing model called the capital asset pricing model (CAPM) says that managers should use only the market risk because investors can eliminate the unique risk. This market risk is captured by a statistic called beta that measures how a company's stock price moves relative to the market as a whole, as measured by, say, the Standard & Poor's 500 index—the market average. A beta of 1.0 means that when the Standard & Poor's 500 goes up (down) by 2 percent, the stock is also expected to go up (down) by 2 percent. Any change in the stock price of more or less than this 2 percent is due to factors unique to the company and will be offset by unrelated moves in other stocks in the investor's portfolio. Stocks with betas greater than 1.0 are more risky than the average stock; stocks with betas less than 1.0 are less risky.

Figure 4-2 contains betas for several U.S. companies. Here is how a manager would use them to estimate what investors require in the way of a return on the equity capital they have committed to the company.

The manager first finds the yield on long-term government bonds from a financial newspaper or Web page. On July 5, 2001, it was 5.42 percent. This is the nominal risk-free interest rate RF. Next, the manager estimates what the risk premium should be for a well-diversified portfolio of common stocks. The risk premium, called the market risk premium, is the return the investor demands in excess of RF. Where does the manager get this number? Well, most managers begin by using the historical difference between the return on a portfolio of large-company stocks (13.2 percent in

FIGURE 4-2   BETAS AND INVESTORS' REQUIRED RATES OF
RETURN FOR THE COMMON STOCK OF SELECTED COMPANIES
JULY 5, 2001

Company	Beta	Risk-free nominal interest rate on long-term government bonds RF	Risk premium RP for stock; RP = (beta)(risk premium for market of 7.50%)	Investors' required rate of return for common stock k k = RF + RP
Kellogg	0.80	5.42%	6.00%	11.42%
PepsiCo	0.90	5.42%	6.75%	12.17%
Merck & Co.	1.20	5.42%	9.00%	14.42%
Dell Computer	1.40	5.42%	10.50%	15.92%

1. Betas will vary by investment advisory services. The betas in this exhibit are from the *Value Line Investment Survey*.
2. The risk-free nominal interest rate is for ten-year U.S. government bonds on July 5, 2001.
3. We have used 7.50% for the market risk premium—the average market premium for 1926 through 1998. Using Dell Computer as an example, we calculate the risk premium as $(1.40)(7.50\%) = 10.50\%$. Many people believe that the market risk premium today is much less than 7.50%. Some would use a number as low as 1.5%. Obviously, a lower market risk premium results in a lower investors' required rate of return.

Figure 4-1) and the average return on long-term government bonds (5.7 percent). This calculation gives a market risk premium of 7.5 percent. Then the manager multiplies the risk premium on the market portfolio by the beta of the company. Let's say the company is Kellogg. Kellogg's beta is 0.80, so Kellogg's required rate of return on its common stock on July 5, 2001, was $5.42\% + 0.80(7.50\%) = 11.42\%$. The required rates of return for the common stocks of the other companies are also listed in Figure 4-2.

What does it mean to say that Kellogg's required rate of return on its common stock is 11.42 percent? It means that Kellogg's managers must earn this return on the investors' equity investment in Kellogg in order to satisfy the investors. If managers fail to earn this return, individual and institutional investors will begin to ask why, and the managers may find themselves replaced and/or their companies restructured.

The major question confronting managers who need to evaluate how the riskiness of a project will affect the company's stock price and future expected cash flows is what to do about unique risk. A company can fail because of unique risk events as well as because of systemic events. For example, investments in research and product development may not pay off, leaving the company in financial distress and the managers and employees without jobs. Yet it may be precisely these investments that are most likely to generate substantial increases in the stock price should they turn out successful new products. Now, the governance question becomes how to get managers and entrepreneurs to make such investments. These problems may well be among the most interesting governance problems for any governance system. We return to them repeatedly throughout the book.

DOES THE CAPM WORK?

Despite the widespread use of the CAPM for estimating required rates of return, the empirical evidence supporting its ability to predict security returns, and hence estimate investors' required rates of return, is weak. Generally speaking, the model underpredicts returns on low-beta stocks and overpredicts returns on high-beta stocks. In other words, the cost of equity capital for low-beta firms, such as Kellogg, is higher than what the CAPM would predict; and the cost of equity capital for high-beta firms, such as Dell Computer, is lower than what the CAPM would predict. More troublesome, though, is the fact that in certain periods some ad hoc models of stock prices do better than the CAPM at explaining historical returns. In particular, size, market-to-book ratios, past performance, price-earnings ratios, and dividend yields have been shown to explain stock returns.

With respect to size, small companies (measured in terms

of their market capitalization, or the market value of their common stock) produced higher returns to investors than large (capitalization) companies. Higher investor returns have also been historically associated with low versus high market-value-to-book-value companies, low relative to high price-earnings ratios, and high relative to low dividend yields. Again translating these findings into equity capital costs, smaller companies, companies with low market-to-book ratios, companies with low price-earnings ratios, and companies with high dividend yields face higher costs of equity capital than their opposites.

Do these findings mean that managers should reject the CAPM as a basis for estimating investors' required rates of returns and evaluating managerial performance? We would caution managers against completely rejecting the CAPM. Underlying the CAPM is a sound financial principle of diversification. Investors clearly can eliminate many of the risks associated with investing in a single company by holding a diversified common stock portfolio. Thus, the idea that investors may be willing to pay more for a portfolio of highly risky companies whose fortunes are not tied to one another than they would pay for a portfolio composed of only one of these highly risky companies remains appealing. What remains to be developed is a model that is better than the current models at telling just how investors do this. Currently, the CAPM (or a variation of it) remains widely used among investors and financial managers, so use it judiciously.

ASSETS IN PLACE VERSUS GROWTH OPPORTUNITIES

An extremely important concept in economics and finance is the opportunity cost of capital. The opportunity cost of capital is the return that investors, including managers who make investment decisions on behalf of shareholders, can earn elsewhere on an infinite number of equally risky alternative investments. For example, investors can buy a large number of very-low-risk corporate bonds—bonds that are rated high quality (AAA) by Moody's and Standard & Poor's. On June 15, 2001, high-quality corporate bonds were yielding 5.50 percent. This 5.50 percent is the opportunity cost of capital facing investors who want to buy AAA-rated bonds. On that date, investors would not buy an AAA bond with less than a 5.50 percent yield because identical bonds offering a higher yield were available. However, suppose an investor discovered an AAA bond offering a 6.60 percent yield. Well, this investor has discovered an asset (the AAA bond) that will earn more than its opportunity cost of capital, and so the investor should snap it up immediately.

Now suppose that instead of AAA bonds, we think in terms of real investments facing managers. Examples would include developing new products and production technologies, expanding product lines, and entering new markets. Now we can talk about the investments that managers make as being those that simply earn their opportunity cost of capital and those that earn more than what would otherwise be available on a wide range of comparably risky investments. (The technical name for these investments is positive net present value investments; we explain this fully in the next chapter.) So, let's return to our stock price valuation model and see what happens when we make some assumptions about whether managers are or are not able to earn more than an investment project's opportunity cost of capital, or what anybody else could earn anywhere else for the same risk.

An Expanded Valuation Model

We can model per share cash dividends (D) as earnings per share (E) multiplied by the factor $(1 - PB)$, where PB repre-

sents the percentage of earnings retained and reinvested in
the company. So, suppose we are looking at Swampy Waters,
Inc., with per share earnings next year (year 1) of $10.00 and
a plowback ratio of 40 percent. Swampy Waters's per share
cash dividend at the end of year 1, therefore, will be $6.00 a
share.

Now the question becomes, What will Swampy earn on
the $4.00 of earnings that it retains and reinvests in the com-
pany? If Swampy's management is able to earn its 20 percent
required return on the $4.00 of retained earnings, earnings
two years from today (year 2) will be $10.00 plus $0.80, or
$10.80. With a plowback ratio of 40 percent, dividends at the
end of year 2 will be $6.48.

Note that dividends go from $6.00 a share in year 1 to
$6.48 in year 2, for a percentage growth rate of 8 percent a
year. This growth rate is exactly equal to the plowback ratio
PB of 40 percent multiplied by the return on investment
ROE of 20 percent. And, with a growth rate of 8 percent,
Swampy Waters's stock will sell for $50.00 a share today.

Okay, suppose that Swampy Waters decides to retain 80
percent of its earnings instead of 40 percent. What will happen to the stock price of the company *today* if it continues
to invest the earnings at 20 percent, its opportunity cost of
capital? Well, the per share cash dividend falls to $2.00, but
the growth rate increases to 16 percent, calculated as
$(80\%)(20\%) = 16\%$. But the stock price stays the same; it is
$50, calculated as

$$P_0 = \frac{\$2.00}{0.20 - 0.16} = \$50$$

Just to emphasize the point, if Swampy pays out all of its
earnings as cash dividends, its per share dividend will be $10,
its growth rate will be 0, and its stock price will still be $50.

The key to understanding why the stock price never

changes is the assumption that Swampy's management can earn only the 20 percent required rate of return on past and new investments. We can show this mathematically by expanding our basic dividend valuation model into

$$P_0 = \frac{D_1}{k-g} = \frac{E_1(1-PB)}{(PB)(ROE)}$$

and, if ROE equals k,

$$P_0 = \frac{D_1}{k-g} = \frac{E_1(1-BP)}{k-(PB)(ROE)} = \frac{E_1(1-PB)}{k-(PB)(k)} =$$

$$\frac{E_1(1-PB)}{k(1-PB)} = \frac{E_1}{k}$$

In other words, for a company earning only its required rate of return, the stock price can be modeled as its earnings per share divided (capitalized) by its investors' required rate of return. For Swampy, this is $10 divided by 20 percent, or $50 a share. This amount is what is called the value of the company's assets in place.

Also note that Swampy's price-earnings (P/E) ratio doesn't change as it changes its plowback ratio. The P/E ratio is always 5, calculated as $50 divided by its per share earnings of $10.

Now, let's suppose that a new manager arrives at Swampy who quickly identifies some projects that have expected rates of return (ROEs) of 30 percent but that still, given their riskiness, have required rates of return of 20 percent—like those AAA bonds with yields way above what is normally available. What happens to the stock price if Swampy's plowback ratio is 60 percent and the earnings are reinvested at 30 percent, for an 18 percent growth rate? Well, the stock price jumps to $200 a share and the P/E ratio becomes 20, calculated as

$$P_0 = \frac{E_1(1-PB)}{k-(PB)(ROE)} = \frac{\$10(1-0.60)}{0.20-(0.60)(0.30)} =$$

$$\frac{\$4.00}{0.20-0.18} = \$200$$

$$PE = \frac{\$200}{\$10} = 20X$$

The difference between the $200 stock price and the $50 assets-in-place stock price is the value of the growth opportunities facing Swampy. This value is effectively equal to the present value of future earnings over and above what would have to be earned to meet the company's 20 percent opportunity cost of capital. Our example also shows why some companies with considerable growth opportunities have much higher P/E ratios than companies with limited growth opportunities.

Figure 4-3 contains a list of stocks where the values have

FIGURE 4-3   VALUE OF ASSETS-IN-PLACE AND GROWTH OPPORTUNITIES FOR SELECTED STOCKS, JUNE 19, 2001

Company	Stock Price June 19, 2001	EPS (First Call)	P/E Ratio	Beta	Investors' Required Rate of Return	Value of Assets in Place	Value of Growth Opportunities
Northeast Utilities	$19.57	$1.62	12.08	0.60	7.70%	$21.04	−$1.47
First Virginia Bank	$45.15	$3.35	13.48	1.00	9.00%	$37.22	$7.93
General Motors	$62.24	$4.66	13.36	1.10	9.325%	$49.97	$12.27
Dell	$24.48	$0.88	27.82	1.30	9.975%	$8.82	$15.66
Pfizer	$43.32	$1.59	27.24	1.10	9.325%	$17.05	$26.27
Amgen	$67.30	$1.42	47.39	0.90	8.675%	$16.37	$50.93

Assumptions: Market risk premium of 3.25%; risk-free rate of 5.75%; long-run market return of 9.00%.

been decomposed into assets in place and growth opportunities. The investors' required rates of return were calculated using the capital asset pricing model. The risk-free interest rate used was 5.75 percent, the rate on long-term U.S. Treasury bonds on June 19, 2001. At the time, many investment analysts and financial economists believed that long-run returns on the stock market would be around 9 percent, so we backed into a market risk premium of 3.25 percent. Our earnings estimates come from First Call and represent consensus estimates of analysts following the companies.

The ratio of the value of growth opportunities to total stock price is low for low-P/E-ratio companies. These companies are usually in mature or regulated industries with limited growth prospects. Note, for example, that Northeast Utilities, based on a 7.70 percent investors' required rate of return, actually has a negative value for growth opportunities, suggesting that the company may experience negative growth or may not earn its required rate of return on future investments.

In contrast, the high-P/E-ratio companies exhibit high ratios of value of growth opportunities to total price. Investors in these companies—Dell, Pfizer, and Amgen—apparently believe that the management will be able to identify and make investments in projects earning more than their opportunity cost of capital.

RELATIVE VALUATION USING COMPARABLES

Practitioners commonly use relative valuation methods rather than absolute valuation models such as the dividend valuation model and the capital asset pricing model. The most commonly used comparable is the P/E ratio. The reliance on comparables goes back to our earlier comments about whether the absolute values of stock prices are reliable indicators of their true value, the difficulty of estimating absolute values, and a general belief that companies that are doing essentially the same thing with the same economic and financial prospects should have comparable values.

For example, companies in the food industry that are of roughly the same size and are selling similar products in similar markets ought to have similar P/E ratios. Figure 4-4 gives these ratios for a number of companies in the food industry. The P/Es range between 14 and 21.

Whether the absolute prices of these companies represent their intrinsic value, however, is another question. All of them could be overpriced or underpriced. And this is the biggest danger of using relative valuations such as P/Es, price to sales, price to book value, and so forth. On a relative basis, the stock may look "fairly" priced. But on an absolute basis, all of the stocks may be badly mispriced.

FIGURE 4-4   P/E RATIOS FOR SELECTED COMPANIES IN THE FOOD PROCESSING INDUSTRY, MAY 2001

Company	Stock Price	Earnings per Share, 2001	P/E Ratio
Campbell Soup	$30.59	$1.65	18.5
General Mills	$40.39	$2.19	18.4
Heinz	$39.28	$2.75	14.3
Hershey Foods	$60.20	$2.75	21.9
Kellogg	$25.58	$1.25	20.5

Source: Value Line, May 11, 2001.

CHAPTER 5

CORPORATE GOVERNANCE ISSUES IN INVESTMENT DECISIONS

INTRODUCTION

In the previous chapter we saw how investors price common stock when they are making investment decisions. Here, we consider the connection between share prices and the investment decisions made by managers using net present value (NPV) analysis and the NPV rule.

Actually, the approach we take is to consider each investment project as a stand-alone independent company. In so
doing, we conceptualize the company as being the sum of its
investment projects—what it does for a living.

THE NPV RULE

Net present value has a precise meaning with respect to the
market value of a company. The NPV of an investment project is the instantaneous change in the market value of the
company that will occur if managers decide to go ahead with
the investment. For example, suppose the NPV of a new
product proposal is $500 million. If investors agree with
management's assessment of the project's benefits, the market value of the company will increase by $500 million as
soon as management announces that it will go ahead with
the new product.

Technically, NPV is defined as the present value of all expected after-tax incremental cash outflows and inflows associated with the project, discounted at the project's risk-
adjusted required rate of return (which is the same as the
project's opportunity cost of capital). And, what amounts to
exactly the same thing, we can also define NPV as the present
value of the expected after-tax cash inflows less the present
value of the expected after-tax cash outflows, with both cash
flow streams discounted at the project's risk-adjusted required rate of return.

Note the close correspondence between this definition and
our definition of stock price, where we said that the stock
price was the present value of the cash flows expected by the
investor, discounted at the investor's risk-adjusted required
rate of return. In effect, the market value of an entirely
equity-financed company (one that has not borrowed any
money) that distributes all after-tax cash flows to sharehold-

ers as cash dividends is simply the sum of the present values of all its current investments in the products and services that it sells for a living. With some modifications, we can show that this definition of the market value of a company's common stock also holds for companies that have used debt to finance themselves and those that reinvest some or all of the current year's after-tax cash flows in new projects.

A Stylized NPV Example

We will use a highly stylized example to demonstrate why managers should use NPV to evaluate investment decisions and how NPV is connected to stock prices. For detailed instructions on how to use NPV and other related techniques for capital budgeting, you should consult a financial management textbook.

The Data

Consider a company called Lamprey Products. Lamprey's management has identified a new product, called Snail Fish. The following information about Snail Fish has been compiled in order to calculate its NPV:

❑ Snail Fish will have a product life of three years; after three years, no one will want to buy any Snail Fish.
❑ Cash sales over the three years are expected to be $600,000 a year.
❑ Cash operating expenses are expected to be $360,000 a year.
❑ Fixed assets costing $300,000 must be bought immediately to produce Snail Fish. The assets will be depreciated over three years at the rate of $100,000 a year for both tax and financial reporting purposes.
❑ The marginal tax rate paid by Lamprey Products is 40 percent.

❏ The risk-adjusted required rate of return on Snail Fish is 14 percent.

The after-tax cash flows for this project appear in Figure 5-1. The major conceptual point to understand is that the project's cash flows are *not* the same as its net income. Observe that for the purpose of calculating net income, the $300,000 cash outlay for equipment is not deducted from revenues in the year it is spent, but instead is spread over the three-year life of the project. This allocation is called depreciation and is a noncash expense. However, depreciation does affect the company's tax liability, and consequently its cash payments for taxes, because it is considered an expense (a

FIGURE 5-1   NPV CALCULATION FOR SNAIL FISH

Item	Year 0	Year 1	Year 2	Year 3
Cash outlay for fixed assets	− $300,000			
Cash revenues		$600,000	$600,000	$600,000
Cash operating expenses		360,000	360,000	360,000
Depreciation (noncash expense)		100,000	100,000	100,000
Net income before taxes (cash revenues less operating expenses and depreciation)		140,000	140,000	140,000
Taxes: 40% of net income paid in cash		56,000	56,000	56,000
Net income after taxes		$84,000	$84,000	$84,000
Cash flows (cash revenues less cash operating expenses and taxes)	− $300,000	$184,000	$184,000	$184,000
Present value of cash flows discounted at 14%	− $300,000	$161,404	$141,582	$124,195
Cumulative present value of cash outflows discounted at 14%	− $300,000			
Cumulative present value of cash inflows discounted at 14%	$427,181			
NPV discounted at 14%	$127,181			

cost) by the Internal Revenue Service. Think of it this way: The $300,000 must be recovered before the project can be said to be profitable—that is, before it generates cash flows in excess of what was spent on the project. The IRS recognizes this and lets you spread this amount over the three-year revenue-generating life of the project.

So, as shown in Figure 5-1, the after-tax cash flows for the project are −$300,000 at time 0 (today) and $184,000 a year for years 1, 2, and 3. Net income before taxes is $140,000 a year for years 1, 2, and 3, and net income after taxes is $84,000. The difference between net income after taxes and cash flow after taxes is the noncash depreciation charge of $100,000 a year, representing the recovery for tax purposes of the initial $300,000 investment.

The Present Values

At a 14 percent required rate of return, the present value of the cash outflows is −$300,000, and that of the cash inflows is $427,181. The NPV is $127,181. The formula for calculating the individual-year present values is

$$PV = \frac{CF_t}{(1 + k)^t}$$

where PV = present value
CF_t = after-tax cash flow in year t
k = investors' required rate of return
t = year t

For example, the calculation for year 2 is

$$PV = \frac{\$184,000}{(1 + 0.14)^2} = \frac{\$184,000}{1.2996} = \$141,582$$

Think of the present values this way: At 14 percent compounded annually, you would need to deposit $124,195 today to have $184,000 three years from today. You would need to deposit $141,582 today to have $184,000 two years from today. And you would need to deposit $161,404 today to have $184,000 one year from today. The present value of the cash inflows, then, is the sum of money you would need to deposit today, invested at 14 percent compounded annually, in order to be able to withdraw $184,000 a year for the next three years, or $427,181. But, lucky you! (Or, we should say, lucky Lamprey shareholders.) Lamprey management has found a way for Lamprey shareholders to withdraw $184,000 a year from the bank called Lamprey Products for a deposit today of only $300,000—the cost of buying the equipment to make Snail Fish.

Interpreting NPV

The difference between what Lamprey must invest in this project and what anyone else would have to invest (put in the bank) to get the same cash flows discounted at the project's required rate of return is called the NPV of the project and is $127,181. We say "what everyone else would have to invest" because the definition of a project's required rate of return is the rate of return that is normally available to everyone on an investment identical to Snail Fish in terms of risk. So, as soon as Lamprey management announces the Snail Fish project to the public, the total market value of Lamprey's common stock will increase by $127,181 to ensure that there are no "money trees" in the stock market that will provide investors with returns greater than fair, competitive risk-adjusted returns. In other words, why would anyone put $427,181 in the bank today in order to withdraw $184,000 a year for the next three years when they could buy the rights to an identical cash flow stream from Lamprey Products for only $300,000 (or $350,000 or $400,000)? Because everybody will want to buy Lamprey Products' stock, the price will rise until it provides the same 14 percent return that you could get everywhere else, which will happen when the total market value of the stock is $427,181.

Now, let's connect these cash flows and market values to the book value of Lamprey Products. To focus on the critical question of market versus book value, let's assume that Lamprey Products has total assets of $300,000, all of these assets are cash, and, Lamprey is an all-equity company (meaning that it has used no debt for financing itself) with 10,000 shares of stock outstanding. By accounting definitions, the total book value of the stockholders' equity is $300,000 and the per share book value is $30. Let's also have the per share stock price equal the per share book value, $30. At this point, the ratio of the market value of the stock to its book value is 1.0. As soon as Lamprey management announces the Snail Fish project, the total market value of the equity jumps to $427,181 and the per share price to $42.7181. The market-value-to-book-value ratio is now 1.424.

When we explore management compensation schemes in Chapter 8, we describe a system called EVA® that ties managerial pay to the ratio of market value to book value. The greater the ratio of market to book, the higher a manager's pay. The rationale for this pay scheme is to align the interests of management with those of the shareholders by rewarding managers for making investment decisions with a positive NPV that increase the company's market-value-to-book-value ratio. The difference between market value and book value is called economic value and is akin to, if not exactly the same as, NPV.

DO INVESTORS BEHAVE AS PREDICTED BY THE NPV RULE?

What evidence is there that investors actually do use cash flows and not net income or short-term earnings per share when they evaluate and price out investment decisions made by management? This question has been examined by many researchers. They have generally found that for companies that announced strategic investment initiatives, the two-day abnormal returns of stock prices increased. Typical findings are that the stock prices of companies that announced major capital expenditures rose by 0.348 percent. For companies that announced new product strategies, the increase was 0.842 percent. For companies that announced substantial increases in research and development expenditures, the increase was 1.195 percent; and for companies that announced joint ventures, it was 0.783 percent.[1] Although these percentages appear to be small, consider that a 0.348 percent increase in the market value of the common stock for, say, Heinz is more than $4.75 million. More important, the stock price reactions were positive, not negative as they would be if investors focused on near-term earnings per share and not future cash flows. All these investments had the effect of lowering the current year's earnings per share relative to what they would otherwise have been, especially the research and development expenditures.

Further evidence supporting the NPV rule as a means for making investment decisions is found in a study by Su Chan, John Kensinger, and John Martin.[2] These researchers carefully examined ninety-five research and development expenditure announcements by companies, which they divided into "high-tech" and "low-tech" companies. They found that the average two-day abnormal return was −1.55 percent for low-tech companies and 2.10 percent for high-tech companies, suggesting that investors reward high-tech research but not low-tech research. Perhaps more important for the question of whether investors take a long-term perspective rather than a short-term earnings perspective is their finding about stock price reactions for companies that announce increases in research and development expenditures at the same time that they announce earning declines. The stock price of these companies increased by 1.01 percent even though they reported earnings decreases.

Subsequent studies continue to confirm these results. On average, strategic investments lead to higher stock prices, regardless of whether the investment is classified by accounting rules as a tangible fixed asset or is an intangible asset that is disguised by accountants as an expense.

IMPLICATION OF THE NPV RULE FOR INTERNAL ALLOCATION OF CAPITAL

The NPV rule has very important implications for the internal allocation of capital among the divisions of a company. Think of each division as a separate company or module, with its own risk and return characteristics and its own present value. Add together the values of the modules and you have the market value of the company. In today's world, where strategists talk about corporate flexibility in terms of putting together or shedding modules, which modules should be kept and which discarded? The answer is: Keep those with positive NPVs and shed those with negative NPVs.

In other words, the NPV rule implies that for allocating capital within the firm (among the modules), investors' risk-adjusted required rates of return should be used as the cost of capital for evaluating projects, both at the divisional level and within divisions or suborganizational units. Divisions with high risk should have high hurdle or discount rates, and divisions with low risk should have low hurdle rates.

Divisions or modules that fail to achieve the required divisional returns should be shut down, spun off, or sold. An example of how one company approaches this internal capital allocation process, with its implications for divestitures and acquisitions, can be found in Quaker Oats Company's 1998 annual report.

Quaker has built its operating and financial strategies around creating economic value. The company states that:

> When we consistently generate and reinvest cash flows [note, cash flows, not net income] in projects whose returns exceed our cost of capital, we create economic value. . . . Value is created when we increase the rate of return on existing capital and reduce investments in businesses that fail to produce acceptable returns over time.

Quaker lists as one of its six operating strategies "improve the productivity of low-return businesses or divest them." It explains this objective by saying:

> Our commitment to deliver shareholder returns that exceed our cost of equity challenges us to achieve a consistent return, better than our cost of capital [meaning positive NPVs] in each of our businesses. In 1998, we divested several businesses that did not meet that objective. During the year we sold Ardmore Farms juices, Continental Coffee, Liqui-Dri biscuits and Nile Spice soup cups for $192.7 million. Although those businesses had approximately $275 million in annualized sales, in total, they were negligible contributors to operating income.[3]

LEGITIMATE AND ILLEGITIMATE CRITICISMS OF THE NPV RULE

Criticisms of the NPV rule and its usefulness for evaluating investment and financing decisions abound. Some are legitimate; others are not. Let's start with some common wrong-headed criticisms.

One of the most common reasons offered for not using NPV is that the project is mandated by health and safety concerns or government regulations. For example, regulations concerning water or air pollution may require the replacement of old equipment with cleaner new equipment. At first glance, such a project seems to fall outside of a NPV analysis because it generates no cash inflows and looks like a negative-NPV investment. However, if the investment is looked at from a more global perspective, the analysis fits quite well into a NPV framework.

What are the consequences of not complying with the pollution control (or, for that matter, occupational safety) regulations? Among those we can think of are fines, the inability to attract and retain high-quality employees and managers, and severe public relations problems, leading to boycotts and loss of sales and reputation. Properly handled in a NPV analysis, these fines and other "costs" would be translated into negative after-tax cash flows if the company did not undertake the required investments. Therefore, the incremental cash flows from the project are the fines and other losses that the company does *not* incur as a result of making investments that reduce pollution and improve working conditions.

Another way to think about this problem is to ask whether the owners of the company would be better off if the company were liquidated rather than making the regulatory required investments. Again, the comparison is not to an existing mode of operation that cannot be maintained, but to the future cash flows should the investments not be undertaken.

Another common criticism of the NPV approach is that it doesn't take qualitative factors such as employee responses to major organizational changes into consideration. We would argue that the problem here is not with the NPV method but with the cash flows used in the calculations. The cash flows have not included the organization costs that the project will impose on the firm.

So, what are some legitimate reasons for not using the NPV rule, or at least not using it in the basic form? Perhaps the best reason for being extremely careful about using the NPV rule when making strategic investment decisions is that these decisions often contain options that will allow the firm to capitalize on future opportunities or to abandon a strategic investment if, with the passage of time and the accumulation of information, it turns out to be not quite what the company expected.

Strategic Options and the NPV Rule

Recall the question we asked in Chapter 3 about whether managers should consider only market (systematic, nondiversifiable) risk or total risk when making investment decisions. There, we said that most of the company's stakeholders would suffer substantial costs regardless of the reason why the firm failed. Thus, managers would be well advised to consider not only the market risk but also the unique risks of any investment—in other words, the total risk.

For example, the employees of a company have a considerable interest in its success because they would incur substantial adjustment costs were the firm to fail. These costs go beyond the costs of looking elsewhere for employment, especially for highly skilled technical and managerial employees. These individuals typically make major commitments of time and effort to develop company-specific skills and look to the continued growth and success of the company for returns on these investments. These returns are not entirely pecuniary, but also come in the form of promotions, status, and job security. So, firms that can offer their employees and managers security and the prospect of financial success are likely to garner greater employee loyalty and to be able to recruit and retain the "better" workers and managers.

But perhaps there is a more fundamental relationship between the survival of the firm and having employees and other stakeholders make firm-specific investments. We would argue that it is the firm-specific skills amassed by the firm's employees that make it possible for the firm to earn quasi rents. Expressed in the terminology of financial management, these firm-specific skills enable the firm to find and undertake projects with a positive net present value.

In other words, from a companywide perspective, new strategic positive NPV investments arise out of past strategic investments and what the company already does for a living. For example, had Pfeiffer Vacuum's previous investments in, say, developing high-technology vacuum equipment for extracting air from potato chip bags not been made, the opportunity for developing the high-technology vacuum processes needed for manufacturing semiconductors would probably not have existed. Therefore, when Pfeiffer Vacuum is considering new strategic investments in vacuum production technology, it needs to consider not only the cash flows from the particular technology or equipment under analysis, but also the value of future options for new products and new markets (say, China or Brazil).

Competitive Analysis Approach

What about the situation facing a division of a company that manufactures products that are also produced by a number of competitors, such as Boeing? Boeing designs, produces, and sells commercial aircraft. Should Boeing continue to do so, and how might Boeing determine whether introducing a wide-bodied aircraft seating 1,000 people is a positive NPV project? An approach frequently found in the management literature is the competitive analysis approach (CAA).

Fundamentally, CAA is a disguised version of the NPV rule that assumes that all competitors are wealth maximizers. We say this because, by definition, a positive NPV project is one whose expected returns are greater than what anyone could earn elsewhere on an equally risky investment. So, for the wide-bodied aircraft to be a positive NPV project for Boeing, Boeing must have some competitive advantage(s) in designing, producing, and selling the aircraft compared to its competitors. If it does not, Boeing is looking at an investment that will leave its stock price, at best, unchanged. So, for Boeing to have a positive NPV on this investment, it must come to the table with a lower cost of capital, better management skills with respect to designing and producing wide-bodied aircraft, and/or other capabilities that its competitors do not possess.

But suppose the governance objective of Boeing's competitors is not shareholder wealth maximization? Now, even though Boeing knows that it has advantages over its competitors, moving ahead with the project on the basis of CAA could still produce a negative NPV outcome. How? Well, Boeing's competitors may be subsidized by their governments or may be operating in corporate governance environments that place shareholder concerns below economywide employment and income priorities. In such a case, using CAA to evaluate investment decisions may lead to Boeing's demise unless it can convince the state of Washington or the federal government to provide similar subsidies.

We used Boeing as an example because its main competitor is Airbus, a consortium of European companies. Historically, some of these companies were at least partially owned by national governments, and Airbus managers were often required to consider the political needs of the consortium members with respect to spreading employment around the various countries when making production decisions.

Another problem with CAA is that it is susceptible to

herding decisions. Suppose some new technological means for selling goods and services is created—say e-commerce. This discovery generates a rapid expansion of firms in the e-commerce business. You do a CAA of your proposed e-commerce project and identify a number of competitive advantages for your firm. Does this mean that you have identified a positive NPV project? Not necessarily. Perhaps the industry, as a whole, is really unprofitable. In this case, you may survive longer than others or lose less money, but you haven't created long-term value for your shareholders.

CHAPTER 6

CORPORATE GOVERNANCE ISSUES AND THE FINANCING DECISION

INTRODUCTION

Financing decisions are concerned with how managers raise the funds needed to operate the company. From an accounting or financial statement perspective, the financing methods chosen appear on the liabilities and shareholders' equity portion of the balance sheet and include bank loans, bonds, capitalized leases, preferred stock, retained earnings, and common stock.

The financing decision is important from a corporate governance perspective because the financial contracts written between the company and the suppliers of capital establish who controls the company and how this control changes if the corporation fails to honor its financial obligations. Just as important, these contracts are used to mitigate conflicts of interests among the stakeholders of the firm. As we've said before, corporate governance is about how the suppliers of capital make sure that they earn a return on the funds placed under the control of managers and make sure that the managers and other stakeholders don't take the money and run.

Financial economists have come a long way in their thinking about financing decisions, a journey that began in the 1950s. At that time, everyone knew that some firms used a lot of debt and others used very little or none. Also, it was apparent that the relative amounts of debt and equity, called financial leverage, also differed by industry. However, no one had really constructed a "scientific" explanation of why and how financial leverage was related to the market value of the company. Thus, the early investigative work focused on questions of market valuation rather than on corporate governance and financial contracting issues and produced a theory of financial leverage under what are called perfect capital market conditions.

We begin with an intuitive explanation of this theory—work for which its developers, Franco Modigliani and Merton Miller, received the Nobel Prize in Economics. The essence of their theory is that in perfect capital markets, the financial decision is irrelevant. But this is not the really interesting prediction made by the theory. The interesting predictions follow from releasing the rigid perfect market assumptions and letting us view financing and financial structure decisions as essentially governance issues with respect to controlling conflicts of interest among corporate stakeholders.

THE SETUP

Think about a company, AlsterLakes, that requires $100 million of capital to operate in a world with no taxes. The company has four owners, and they can put the $100 million into the company in two ways: equity (common stock) or debt (bonds). However, we are going to insist on the following rule: Every owner must contribute capital with the same proportions of debt and equity. In other words, if, collectively, the owners decide to contribute $40 million in debt and $60 million in equity, each owner must hold the same ratio of debt to equity. For example, owner A would have $20 million in debt and $30 million in equity, owner B would have $4 million in debt and $6 million in equity, and so on.

Now, let us further suppose that this company generates $20 million in cash (call it earnings before interest payments) for distribution to the investors. Owner A owns 50 percent of the debt and 50 percent of the equity; therefore, owner A has a claim to 50 percent of the $20 million, or $10 million. Owner B owns 10 percent of the debt and 10 percent of the equity and thus has a claim to 10 percent of the $20 million, or $2 million. Does (should) either owner care whether the cash flows come as interest payments or cash dividend payments as long as both are taxed identically at the personal level? Most likely, the answer is no. So, why should the total market value of the debt and equity—the market value of the company—be affected by the way the investors financed the company?

Let's now make things a bit more realistic and introduce a corporate tax code in which interest expense is deductible for tax purposes but cash dividend payments are not. We'll keep the debt at $40 million, assume an 8 percent interest rate on the debt ($3.2 million a year), and impose a 40 percent tax rate. Of course, less than $20 million will now be available to distribute to the investors because of taxes, but how much less? The amounts available with different levels of debt are shown in Figure 6-1.

The line to focus on in Figure 6-1 is the bottom line, which shows the total of interest payments and net income after taxes. Remember, everyone who has put money into this company has a proportionate share of this total. So, if the company has $40 million in debt, the investors get to distribute $13.28 million among themselves. This amount is considerably more than the $12 million that the investors would have received had they put all their money into the company in the form of equity. Thus, it looks as if one way to increase the market value of the company is to use debt financing because of the deductibility of interest expense. But if $40

FIGURE 6-1   CASH AVAILABLE FOR DISTRIBUTION TO INVESTORS (SECURITY HOLDERS) UNDER DIFFERENT AMOUNTS OF DEBT FINANCING FOR ALSTERLAKES (MILLIONS OF DOLLARS)

	$0	$20	$40	$60	$80
Debt	$0	$20	$40	$60	$80
Equity	$100	$80	$60	$40	$20
Total Capital	**$100**	**$100**	**$100**	**$100**	**$100**
EBIT	**$20.0**	**$20.0**	**$20.0**	**$20.0**	**$20.0**
Interest (8%)	0	$1.6	$3.2	$4.8	$6.4
Net income before taxes	20.0	$18.4	$16.8	$15.2	$13.6
Taxes at 40%	8.0	7.36	6.72	6.08	5.44
Net income after taxes	$12.0	$11.04	$10.08	$9.12	$8.16
Interest plus net income after taxes available for investors	**$12.0**	**$12.64**	**$13.28**	**$13.92**	**$14.56**

million in debt is so much better than no debt, why not $80 million? Well, for one thing, because the Internal Revenue Service (IRS) monitors this sort of behavior and will eventually step in and declare that the debt is really equity and what you are doing is simply avoiding the payment of taxes.

Setting aside IRS compliance issues, though, what we observe is that as long as the *same* people own both the debt (bondholders) and the equity (shareholders) of a company, the more debt that is used, the more cash exists after taxes for distribution to the investors. But suppose the bondholders and the shareholders are *not* the same people? Well, here is where the governance issues emerge and the financing decision becomes interesting, because now conflicts of interest arise in a world in which people act in their own self-interest and some people have more information than other people (technically described as informational asymmetries).

Shareholder/Bondholder Conflicts of Interest

Suppose the investors who buy the bonds of AlsterLakes are not the same people who buy the stock. Now we can no longer say that the investors will be indifferent with respect to the distribution of cash flows from the company. Legally, the bondholders have priority over the shareholders with respect to their claims on the cash flows. Before any dividend payments can be made to the shareholders, the creditors must receive their interest and principal payments. Consequently, as the firm takes on more and more debt, creditors become more and more concerned about the likelihood of their receiving their interest and principal payments. Creditors also become concerned about a number of other possible events in a world where owner/managers have more information about the company than the creditors and where owner/managers are interested in maximizing their wealth, not that of the bondholders. Among these other events are:

1. Changing the investment strategy from low-risk to high-risk investments
2. Gambling on high-risk negative NPV projects to escape bankruptcy
3. Selling assets and distributing cash without paying down debt
4. Selling new debt that has the same priority as existing debt

The Events

The first event goes by the name of *risk shifting*. Alster-Lakes tells creditors that it needs the money to buy equipment for manufacturing widgets, then uses the money to explore for oil in New Hampshire. The risks of oil exploration in New Hampshire are considerably greater than the risks of manufacturing widgets, even if the oil exploration project has a positive expected return. Thus, creditors need to protect themselves against such opportunistic behavior.

The second item on the list is most likely to happen in companies that are facing financial problems. Suppose Alster-Lakes begins losing money and the management starts looking around for other projects to invest in. The managers can't find any projects that can earn the company's cost of capital, but they have identified a project, MegaLottery, that has some very high possible payoffs even though it has a negative expected value (negative NPV). The managers decide to invest in MegaLottery because if they invest in MegaLottery and the investment fails or if they don't invest, they will be out of a job and the shareholders will lose their investment in the company. But if the managers invest in MegaLottery, they have a chance of getting a lucky draw and surviving.

The third item is also known as "taking the money and running." Rather than build up cash to make future interest and principal payments, the owner/managers distribute the cash as dividends. The result is cash leaving the company and a deterioration in the creditors' position.

The fourth item describes situations in which owner/managers borrow, say, $100 million from one group of creditors and informally promise not to borrow any more money. However, the owner/managers then violate that promise and borrow another $50 million from another lender, giving the second lender the same priority in cash flows as the first group of creditors. Creditors worry about these tricky deals also.

How Creditors Protect Themselves with Covenants

Creditors protect themselves against these potential events by including covenants in debt contracts that prevent owner/managers from doing certain things and/or require them to do other things. The first are called negative covenants; the second, positive covenants.

Creditors use negative covenants to prevent borrowers from changing financing, investment, and dividend policies that were announced, implied, or promised at the time the funds were borrowed. For example, restrictions may be placed on minimum net worth, additional debt financing, dividend payments, and share repurchases. The company may also be prevented from selling assets and distributing the proceeds to shareholders.

Creditors can require specific collateral for their loans, usually the asset for which the loan was made, and can prohibit the borrower from pledging the collateral for other loans. Creditors can also specify that their claims to interest and principal payments take priority over the claims of new creditors.

Positive covenants require the firm to pursue certain specific policies, usually of a financial nature. The most common positive covenant requires the borrower to furnish financial statements to the lender—information that the lender uses to monitor the borrower. Depending on the strength of the borrower and the competitive position of the lender, additional positive covenants may be included. These would include minimum interest coverage ratios and liquidity ratios.

Failure of the borrower to comply with the covenants places the borrower in technical default on the loan, allowing the lender to demand immediate payment. Lenders are unlikely to do so; instead, they will work with the company to restructure the loan. But, ultimately, the lenders will gain effective control of the company and become its new owners if the borrower is unable to satisfy their demands or requirements for restructuring the original lending agreement.

Shareholder/Manager Conflicts of Interest

From a corporate governance perspective, the financing decision can be and is used to control conflicts of interest between shareholders and managers and to focus managerial attention on shareholders' concerns. Figure 6-2 contains a summary of abnormal stock price returns after announcements of financing, investment, and dividend decisions. The events are divided into two categories: cash flows from the firm to investors and cash flows from investors to the firm. Positive abnormal returns are associated with cash flows to the investors, and negative returns are associated with cash flows from investors to the firm. Investment increases are regarded as increases in cash flows to investors because they are assumed to be investments in positive NPV projects that will yield increased cash flows in the future. Financial economists have a theory that explains these abnormal returns. It is called the free cash flow theory and is rooted in conflicts of interest between managers and shareholders.

Free cash flow is the cash remaining after all debt and lease

FIGURE 6-2   TWO-DAY ABNORMAL COMMON STOCK PRICE RETURNS AFTER ANNOUNCEMENTS ABOUT CASH FLOWS BETWEEN THE COMPANY AND CAPITAL MARKETS OR INVESTORS

Cash Flow Event	Two-Day Abnormal Percentage Returns
Increases in cash flows to the investor	
Common stock repurchases	
Tender offers	16.2%
Open-market purchases	3.6
Dividend increases	
Dividend initiation	3.7
Dividend increase	0.9
Special dividend	2.1
Investment increases	1.0
Decreases in cash flows to the investor	
Security sales	
Common stock	− 1.6
Preferred stock	0.1
Convertible preferred	− 1.4
Straight debt	− 0.2
Convertible debt	− 2.1
Dividend decreases	− 3.6
Investment decreases	− 1.1

Source: Clifford W. Smith, Jr., "Raising Capital: Theory and Evidence," *Midland Corporate Finance Journal* (Spring 1986), pp. 6–11.

obligations have been met and the investments necessary to maintain the core activities of the business have been made. The cash that is left over can either be returned to the shareholders as cash dividends or be kept in the company. The important question is: What should the managers do with this cash if no profitable investment opportunities have been identified? The short answer is, return it to the shareholders.

However, managers may be reluctant to lose control over this cash. Management compensation, power, and status are frequently related to the size of the firm rather than to the performance of its stock price. Thus, managers may find it advantageous to "grow the firm" beyond the size that maximizes shareholders' wealth. For example, a *Wall Street Journal* story about Coca-Cola's very large layoffs in January 2000 noted that "[Coke's] board had grown tired of watching profits swallowed up by a bureaucracy and staffing that ballooned the company to 30,000 employees during Coke's glory days of the last decade."[1] In this instance, outside board members stepped in to force changes, a role and rationale for outside directors that we return to in a later chapter.

Other stakeholders in the firm will often support managerial strategies that grow the firm at the expense of the shareholders. Employees are loath to see their jobs disappear, and local politicians will not want to see local operations curtailed because these operations generate jobs and tax revenues.

Stockholders are aware of these conflicts of interest. Therefore, shareholders seek ways to limit managerial discretion over the use of free cash flow and reduce agency costs. One way to remove managerial control over free cash flow is to use debt financing. With debt financing, more cash is needed for interest and principal payments; therefore, there is less cash available for growing the firm at the expense of the shareholders. In addition, some would argue that the increased fixed charges for interest and principal payments motivate managers to run the company more efficiently so as to be certain of being able to make the payments. Other ways to remove cash are to pay cash dividends or repurchase common stock. Georgia-Pacific, for example, says, "There may be periods when the Georgia-Pacific Group generates cash in excess of opportunities for investment. If debt is below the target level set by the Board of Directors, cash will be returned to our shareholders through share repurchases, so they can make their own investment choices."[2]

Note that the free cash flow story we have just presented is a corporate governance explanation of why firms use debt. According to this argument, the reason debt is used is to control stakeholders' attempts to transfer wealth from the owners to others; the purpose is not to lower the cost of financing the company, although that may be one of the side effects that comes out of the process.

The Financing Decision and Customers

Suppose you are shopping for a round-trip ticket to Florida to escape Chicago's windy and snowy winter. You know that you will have to purchase the ticket in September, as you may find it difficult to obtain reservations at the time you want to go or to obtain them at a reasonable price if you wait until January. You can choose from a number of airlines, including Atlantic Skyways and Air White Pine.

You frequently hear that Atlantic Skyways is having financial difficulties and that investment analysts are forecasting an impending bankruptcy for the company, in part because of large amounts of debt in its capital structure. Air White Pine, however, is financially healthy, with comparatively little debt and a history of profitable operations. Both airlines charge the same fare. Which airline do you choose?

We suspect that you will book your flight on Air White Pine. Why take the risk that four months from now, in January, Atlantic won't be around to fly you to Orlando, that your originally scheduled flight will be canceled, or that the flight will be overbooked so that Atlantic can collect more cash from prepaid tickets? We suspect that others will reach the same conclusion.

The consequence for Atlantic of these consumer decisions is that advance ticket sales decline, thereby depriving Atlantic of the very cash it needs in order to survive. Of course, Atlantic may try to alleviate its competitive weakness by offering lower fares than Air White Pine, but this means lower profits.

Our point is that customers are very interested in a company's financial position and whether the company can deliver on its implied contracts with the customers if they pay for a product or service prior to receiving it. Product warranties on new cars fall into this category, as does the provision of technical services for computer equipment and software for the computer system. Indeed, SAP, the German software company, adopted U.S. accounting rules because "When people buy SAP, smart people look at the financial strength of the company selling the software. You could buy the hottest software, but if the company selling it goes bankrupt, you have no support. You're stranded."[3]

The Financing Decision and Employees

Another assumption of the "capital structure doesn't matter" story is that there is no connection between the firm's labor market and the way the firm is financed. However, people are attracted to firms that offer employment security and prospects for personal development and growth. Therefore, firms that are in financial distress are less able than financially strong firms to attract, motivate, and retain employees.

The connections between labor markets and financial structure are strongest in those firms where employees invest in and gain firm-specific knowledge—skills and knowledge that cannot be easily transferred to jobs at other companies. Such skills include the ability to maintain and repair firm-specific machinery, knowledge of informal organizational structures, and team relationships for product development.

This relationship between financing, governance systems,

and employees carries over into employee compensation schemes. One advantage of a public corporation whose shares are traded on financial markets is that it can use high-powered incentive systems to compensate employees. Typically, high-powered incentive plans involve stock ownership and/or rights to buy stock, called stock options. To offer employees such a plan, the company must have publicly traded stock outstanding—stock that can be valued by independent investors in the marketplace. In other words, in order to provide high-powered incentive plans for employees and managers, a company's governance structure is likely to include public shareholders. Indeed, one might argue that market-based governance structures are an important ingredient for a society that wants to encourage economic growth through innovation.

BANK DEBT VERSUS PUBLIC DEBT

Does it matter whether a firm uses bank debt or public debt, where public debt means selling bonds in the capital markets? In other words, are the governance implications different depending on who provides the debt financing?

The answer is yes. Corporations can usually sell bonds at lower interest rates than they would have to pay for bank debt. Furthermore, bank debt usually contains more of the positive and negative covenants that we mentioned earlier than bonds do. But these advantages of public debt come at a cost. Should the corporation get into financial difficulty, it will find it easier to rewrite debt contracts with banks than to rewrite those with public bondholders. This situation faced Bethlehem Steel in July 2001. Bethlehem Steel got waivers of its net worth requirements from its banks to enable it to find ways of coping with very competitive market conditions. The company also received waivers from other lenders, and the

lenders to two of its joint venture partners agreed not to en-
force their rights against Bethlehem Steel, which had guaran-
teed the partners' loans.[4] So, the question of bank (private)
versus public (bonds) debt is another governance problem in
terms of how suppliers of capital to a company make sure
that they are repaid and how the borrowers are controlled by
the lenders.

Not everybody likes banks, however. For example, here's
what Henning Kagermann, joint chairman of SAP in 1998,
had to say about banks: "From the beginning we [SAP]
sought to be independent of banks. That gave us flexibility
and freedom. There were no big banks telling us what to do."
As far as Kagermann is concerned, any benefits associated
with a lower cost of capital arising from financial leverage
are more than offset by the governance problems of bank
financing.[5]

Kagermann's attitude is not unusual. As firms become
larger, they seek to diversify their sources of debt funds in
order to gain more discretion over their investment decisions
and more bargaining power with their fund suppliers. For
corporate managers, this diversification of funding sources
means not only using more banks, but also escaping banks
by selling bonds.

Financial economists have compiled some interesting evidence about how bank debt and financing with bonds instead of bank debt affect stock prices. The evidence is
consistent with the idea that public shareholders view banks
as (shareholder) delegated monitors of management and the
financial situation of the company.[6]

The IPOs of companies with banking relationships sell for
a higher price than the IPOs of companies with no banking
relationships.[7] The banks, it seems, provide a seal of approval
on the IPO for public investors. A company's stock price also
rises whenever a company renews or renegotiates its loans
with a bank, so long as the terms of the loan remain the same

or are improved. Furthermore, the better the credit rating of the bank, the more positive the reaction of the company's stock price. This positive stock price reaction stands in contrast to negative stock price reactions when a company announces a public bond issue.

As for our assertion that it is easier to recontract with a bank than with public bondholders, consider the following evidence: When a firm announces that it will borrow funds from a syndicate of banks (more than one bank), the reaction of the company's stock price depends on the number of banks in the syndicate. For up to three banks, a positive reaction is observed; beyond three banks, there is no reaction. The explanation could be that as more and more banks become part of the syndicate, the bank loan becomes more and more like a public bond issue because as the number of lenders increase, it becomes more and more difficult to renegotiate loan terms.[8]

We close this section by pointing out that conflicts of interest exist between banks and public bondholders. Suppose a company that runs into financial difficulty has both public and private debt outstanding. What motivation does the bank have for renegotiating a loan if all of the benefits flow to the public bondholders? The effect of using public debt, then, has been to increase the likelihood that, should the company run into difficulty, the bank will take a firmer stance and will extract greater concessions from the shareholders.

DOES WHERE YOU RAISE FUNDS MATTER?

Where firms finance themselves and whether they use public or private sources of capital also seems to matter. SAP, the

German software company, listed its shares on the New York Stock Exchange in 1998. One of the major reasons given was that the NYSE listing would broaden the potential market for its shares among institutional investors. Pfeiffer Vacuum noted that listing on the NYSE would result in shareholders who valued high-technology ventures and who understood the business better than domestic German investors did.

Ulrich Hartmann, chairman of the board of VEBA, a German company that listed itself on the NYSE in 1997, had this to say:

> We are also vitally interested in tapping the U.S. market for ideas—to bolster our continuous process of corporate reform. After our stock market listing, we will be better able to absorb ingredients of the U.S. business and management culture that are necessary for Germany's success. . . . With our listing, we are deliberately exposing ourselves to the critical appraisal of the world's most important capital market. And we hope to expand our access to U.S. institutional funds.[9]

The quote from VEBA is especially interesting from a governance perspective. In effect, VEBA wanted to tap the U.S. markets not because doing so would be cheaper but because it provided a way of monitoring, disciplining, and controlling managers—a governance objective.

CHAPTER 7

CORPORATE GOVERNANCE DIVIDEND ISSUES

INTRODUCTION

Why do firms pay cash dividends? Why do firms that pay cash dividends follow what is called a constant dollar growth rate policy whenever possible? And, most important, what is the connection, if any, between cash dividends, dividend policy, and corporate governance systems?

The thinking of financial economists about dividend policy and why firms pay cash dividends has evolved in much the same way as their thinking about financing the company. Initially, economists focused on whether any connection existed between dividend policy and the firm's cost of capital or, which is essentially the same thing, its market value. This analysis was carried out under the same perfect capital market assumptions that we noted in the description of financing decisions. But, as empirical evidence about the relationship between firm value and cash dividends began to accumulate, dividend policy increasingly came to be seen as another means of mitigating conflicts of interest among the stakeholders of the firm.

As in the previous chapter, we set up the issues by asking what would be the dividend policy of a company operating in a world in which there were no taxes and no conflicts of interest among the firm's stakeholders. We then introduce the governance problems associated with self-seeking behavior on the part of managers, who have more information about the company than the public shareholders do. We conclude with a brief description of the apparent connection between dividend policy and different corporate governance and national legal systems.

THE SETUP: WHY PAY CASH DIVIDENDS?

Managers can do two things with current year's earnings: They can distribute them as cash dividends, or they can retain them in the company. If the earnings are retained, management can use them to make additional investments or to pay down debt. The decision to pay down debt is part of the financing decision and is connected to the notion of an optimal capital structure and solving governance problems through the financial structure decision. So, setting aside the "pay down the debt" alternative, when should management retain earnings and reinvest them in the company, and when should management distribute the earnings as cash dividends?

Arguably, the best reason for paying cash dividends is that management knows that no positive NPV investments exist for the firm. Therefore, rather than keeping cash in the company, where it earns no return, the managers should distribute it to the owners of the company as cash dividends. The owners of the company can then use these cash dividend payments to invest in other companies that have positive NPV projects available to them. Thus, they would be able to create jobs and economic growth for the economy as a whole were they to receive the funds—essentially the public policy objective of a well-functioning corporate governance system. This theory is called the *residual theory of cash dividends*.

If corporations were actually following this policy, though, we would observe much more volatility in year-to-year cash dividend payments than we do in reality—volatility that would be more akin to that observed in net income and earnings per share. However, as shown in Figure 7-1, dividends per share are very stable from one year to the next in the face of substantial earnings volatility. Furthermore, cash dividends per share can even go up in a year when earnings go down. Why?

SOLVING INFORMATIONAL ASYMMETRY PROBLEMS

If you are a stockholder in Willamette Industries, how much information do you have about its worldwide operations and its competitors? How much can you really find out about its future prospects by reading current financial statements or, these days, Web page message boards?

Figure 7-1   Earnings per Share (EPS) and Dividends per Share (DPS) for Selected Companies

	Arvin Industries		Cooper Industries		Willamette Industries	
Year	EPS	DPS	EPS	DPS	EPS	DPS
1999	$3.65	$0.85	$3.50	$1.32	$1.70	$0.72
1998	3.23	0.81	2.47	1.32	0.80	0.64
1997	2.66	0.77	3.16	1.32	0.66	0.64
1996	1.61	0.76	2.72	1.32	1.74	0.62
1995	1.24	0.76	2.41	1.32	4.67	0.57
1994	1.85	0.76	2.10	1.32	1.62	0.48
1993	1.81	0.76	2.75	1.32	1.07	0.44
1992	1.70	0.70	2.71	1.24	0.76	0.42
1991	0.75	0.68	3.01	1.16	0.45	0.40

One way for management to answer questions about the future prospects and fundamental health of the company is to send you multicolor brochures, appear at analysts meetings, and issue press releases. However, management's interpretation of the data may differ considerably from other versions, especially those that shareholders might develop if they had access to the same information as management. Furthermore, given managers' self-interest in the survival of the firm and their tenure as employees, to what extent should public shareholders trust management to be forthright with them about the company's prospects and financial position?

A better way for management to communicate information about the company's prospects and financial position is to send cash dividend checks. Much less interpretation is necessary. For example, in its 2000 annual report, the management of Genuine Parts Company says:[1]

We are proud of our dividend record, which has been successfully supported by earnings through the years and our dividends in 2000 were $1.10 a share. On February 19, 2001, the Board of Directors increased the cash dividend payable April 2, 2001 to an annual rate of $1.14 per share, an increase of 4%. This equals 52% of our 2000 earnings and becomes our 45th consecutive year of dividend increases.

By making cash payments, Genuine Parts's management is not only communicating information about the company but also making a covenant with the stockholders. Management makes an implicit promise to continue these payments unless the fundamental financial position of the company changes. Look at it this way: The fact that cash dividend payments must be made with cash means that managers of firms that are in financial difficulty today or are likely to run into difficulty in the future cannot imitate the cash dividend payments of good companies without sustaining costs. They don't have the cash to make the payments, and if, as a result, they have to reduce dividends from their previous level, shareholders can act to replace the managers with new ones. So, managers use cash dividend payments to communicate information about the company to its shareholders, especially about the fundamental health of the company.

Look at the year-to-year earnings per share changes for Willamette Industries in Figure 7-1. In 1997, earnings per share fell to $0.66 from $1.74 in 1996. Yet, management actually increased dividends from $0.62 to $0.64 a share. In effect, management was saying that the sharp reduction in earnings was a transitory event and that, from a longer-term perspective, the company was in excellent shape.

By the same token, the sharp earnings increase to $4.67 a

share in 1995 from $1.62 in 1994 was associated with a very small increase in cash dividends. Here, management was saying, don't get overly excited about this big earnings jump; it's not going to happen year after year. So, from a governance perspective, it is possible to think of dividend policy as solving problems of information flows between owners and managers.

DIVIDENDS, FREE CASH FLOW, AND CONFLICTS OF INTEREST

Recall that free cash flow is the cash remaining after all debt and lease obligations have been serviced and positive NPV investments related to the company's current operations have been funded. Under the residual theory of cash dividends, this free cash flow would be distributed to the shareholders as cash dividends.

However, as we noted earlier, managers are reluctant to lose control over this cash. Managerial compensation, power, and status are frequently related to firm size. Therefore, managers may find it advantageous to "grow the firm" beyond the size that maximizes shareholder value. Even more important, managers may seek to ensure that the firm survives as an entity, especially if it is in a declining industry. Cash dividends, therefore, are a way of removing free cash flow from managerial control in firms that face limited investment opportunities.

Dividends and Growth Opportunities

Think about the kinds of firms that are most likely to face limited investment opportunities and those that are most likely to face unlimited or at least a lot of favorable investment opportunities (positive NPV projects). Typically firms in mature and declining industries will have limited investment opportunities, whereas firms in new and expanding industries will see many such opportunities—let's call them growth opportunities. So, shareholders of firms with growth opportunities will be much less concerned about whether the managers of these companies are making negative NPV investments than will shareholders of firms in mature industries. The result will be (and is) that the percentage of earnings paid out as cash dividends by firms in mature industries is greater than that for firms in growth industries, provided governance structures are in place that encourage or force the managers of firms that are hoarding cash to disgorge that cash and return it to the shareholders. And here is a major governance issue: How do shareholders of these firms get managers to disgorge the cash?

We turn to these questions in the next three chapters, where we consider managerial pay schemes, the market for corporate control, and the role and composition of the board of directors. Anticipating these chapters, however, for the cash to be disgorged, managerial pay must be connected to share price performance, a market for corporate control must exist, and laws protecting the public investor must exist.

Dividends and Legal Systems

A recent survey of dividend policies around the world lends support to the notion that the combination of governance structures and laws protecting the rights of minority shareholders (small public investors) affects dividend policy. The authors divided countries into civil-law countries and common-law countries because common-law countries have stronger investor protection laws than civil-law countries. Common-law countries (Australia, Canada, United Kingdom, United States) are also more likely to have market-based Anglo-American governance systems than civil-law countries (France, Germany, Japan, South Korea). The authors then divided the publicly traded corporations in these countries into companies with growth opportunities and mature companies facing limited growth opportunities. Their findings are shown in Figure 7-2.

The dividend payout ratios of growth companies, measured by growth in sales, were lower than those of mature companies in common-law countries. However, the dividend payout ratios of mature companies in civil-law countries with weak investor protection were significantly lower than those of mature companies in common-law countries that had strong investor protection laws. Therefore, the combination of governance structures and investor protection laws matters in terms of reducing the agency costs and potential misallocation of capital associated with the separation of ownership and management. The authors conclude that "firms appear to pay out cash dividends to investors because the opportunities to steal or misinvest it are in part limited by law, and because minority shareholders have enough power to extract it."[2]

FIGURE 7-2   DIVIDEND PAYOUT RATIOS CLASSIFIED BY LEGAL REGIME AND SALES GROWTH RATES

	Dividend Payout Ratio		
	All Companies	Companies with Higher Than Average Sales Growth	Companies with Lower Than Average Sales Growth
Civil-law countries	27.7%	30.4%	21.3%
Common-law countries	36.3%	28.0%	40.9%
Low investor protection	25.3%	31.3%	21.2%
High investor protection	35.6%	29.0%	39.7%

Adapted from Rafael La Porta, Florencil Lopez-De-Silanes, Andrei Shleifer, and Robert W. Vishny, "Agency Problems and Dividend Policies," *Journal of Finance* 55, February 2000, pp. 1–34.

DIVIDENDS, TAXES, AND SHARE REPURCHASES

A share repurchase refers to the corporation's purchase of its common stock from public shareholders (buying back shares in the secondary market). Financial economists consider share repurchases to be virtually the same as cash dividends. In both cases, the cash leaves the company and goes to the shareholders. The difference is that with a share buyback, investors are effectively given the choice of keeping their shares in the company and receiving no "cash dividend" or selling their shares to the company and receiving cash. If the share repurchase is properly designed, shareholders would be indifferent between selling their shares and keeping them if the tax effects were neutral. However, because capital gains and dividend income are treated differently in the United States and many other countries, some shareholders may prefer a share buyback to a cash dividend as a method for getting excess cash out from under the control of managers.

For example, in the United States, high-income individuals face close to a 40 percent marginal tax rate on cash dividend income but only a 20 percent marginal tax rate on capital gains. Now, suppose Oyster River Corporation, with 10 million shares outstanding, has $50 million in cash that it wants to distribute to its shareholders and the stock price is currently $40 a share, for a market value of the equity of $400 million.

Oyster River could simply declare a $5 per share cash dividend payable to each share. The $50 million would then leave the company, and the stock price would fall to $35 a share. The stock price falls because $50 million has left the company, leaving it with a market value of $350 million. After the cash dividend payment, each shareholder has a share of stock worth $35 and $5 in cash, for a total of $40.

Alternatively, Oyster River could use the $50 million to buy back shares of stock at $40 a share. With $50 million, Oyster River could buy back 1,250,000 shares, leaving 8,750,000 shares outstanding. These shares would now be worth $350 million divided by 8,750,000, or $40 a share. Those who sold their shares back to Oyster River would have $40 in cash, and those who did not sell would have a share worth $40— the same value in either case.

The advantage of the share buyback to the person with a high marginal tax rate is that if she sold the shares, she would pay a capital gains tax, which is a maximum of 20 percent, on the difference between $40 a share and the price she originally paid for the shares. Better yet, if she chose not to sell the shares, she would owe no tax at all because taxes are levied only on actual cash receipts, not paper gains.

Considerable evidence has been accumulated over the years with regard to the effects of share repurchases on stock prices. On average, a company that announces a one-time lump-sum buyback sees its stock price increase by about 20 percent on the announcement day. Companies that announce that they will buy back their shares over time, depending on market conditions, see their stock price go up by about 3 percent on the day the share repurchase program is announced.

AN EXAMPLE OF DISGORGING CASH: FORD MOTOR COMPANY

In May 2000, Ford Motor Company announced that it would spin off its Visteon parts-making unit to Ford shareholders and boost its stock price with a dividend increase and share buyback. In addition to receiving shares in Visteon, Ford shareholders would have the choice of turning in their existing Ford shares for either (1) $20 in cash and new Ford shares or (2) new Ford shares worth the equivalent of option 1. Option 1 would be treated as a share buyback, so the $20 in cash would be taxed as a capital gain. Option 2 would be equivalent to not selling your shares back to Ford and not having to pay any taxes.

At the time of the announcement, Ford had $24 billion of cash reserves, and many analysts considered this amount excessive. Consequently, the company was under pressure from investors to disgorge this cash rather than sitting on it. The decision to disgorge the cash in the form of a share buy-back coupled with a "reissue" of Ford shares was related to the Ford family's desire to retain control of the company and, most likely, the desire of many investors to minimize the tax liability of the distribution. About $10 billion of cash was distributed to shareholders under this plan.

EXPLICIT FREE CASH FLOW DIVIDEND/ SHARE REPURCHASE POLICIES

Georgia-Pacific Corporation offers a textbook example of how managers use share repurchases to distribute free cash flow to shareholders. In a section of the company's 2000 annual report entitled "Excess Cash Returned to Shareholders," management says:

> There may be periods when the Georgia-Pacific Group generates cash in excess of opportunities for investment. If debt is below the target level set by the Board of Directors, cash will be returned to our shareholders through share repurchases so they can make their own investment choices. We believe our

long-term shareholders will benefit as their proportionate ownership of the Georgia-Pacific Group grows.

The company goes on to note that "These share repurchases represent a *tax-efficient* [our italics] distribution . . . to our shareholders [3]

Genuine Parts Company has a similar policy. Genuine Parts, in its 2000 annual report, said that

> We were able to generate $478 million in free cash flow as we continue to focus on this area and improve our return on assets. During the year, the company repurchased approximately 5.5 million shares. . . . We plan to continue our pattern of share repurchases over the coming years while generating enough free cash flow to support this activity and make the necessary investments in the ongoing growth of our business.[4]

CHAPTER 8

CORPORATE GOVERNANCE AND MANAGERIAL COMPENSATION

INTRODUCTION

A major responsibility of the board of directors is to determine managerial compensation systems. How should managers be compensated? Should pay be tied to performance? How should performance be measured? What evidence

117

is there about the relation between managerial pay and performance? What pay, performance evaluation, and compensation systems are likely to mitigate and not exacerbate conflicts of interests between managers and shareholders?

THE PROBLEM

Consider a New Hampshire ski resort, SkiTrails, that is publicly owned. Ownership is dispersed, and the resort is run by a manager. In this arrangement, the manager is the agent of the owners, who want the manager to maximize the market value of SkiTrails. If the owners could directly observe the manager's day-to-day effort and had as much information as the manager about why the financial performance of Ski-Trails was good or bad, they could simply pay the manager a fixed wage and fire him if he shirked, consumed perquisites, or lacked the necessary skills for successfully managing the enterprise. The problem, however, is that the owners cannot directly observe the manager's efforts and that the manager typically has more information than the owners about why SkiTrails is or is not profitable. So, what can the owners do to solve this informational asymmetry problem and get information about whether the manager is putting out adequate effort, where adequate means managing effectively, not shirking, and adding value to the company.

One way to deal with this problem is to tie the manager's compensation entirely to an output measure—let's say profits. For example, the SkiTrails manager could be paid 10 percent of the resort's yearly profits. But this pay scheme creates an additional problem.

Should the manager's pay be affected by events beyond his control? Suppose that a record heat wave hits New Hampshire during November and December, making it impossible to blow snow and operate the mountain. Then, suppose that a dearth of snow is accompanied by a stretch of bitterly cold weather, with wind chills in the minus thirties. As a result of these acts of nature, SkiTrails loses money that year and the manager earns no income, even though, without his efforts, SkiTrails would have gone bankrupt. (For a real example, substitute the dismal performance of technology stocks in 2000 and 2001 for the ski resort.)

Alternatively, suppose the entire ski season is one of sunny, thirty-degree days with six inches of snow every night. Should the manager share in the extraordinary profits of this season? Let's call this weather risk uncontrollable risk.

Perhaps some managers might be willing to take on this uncontrollable risk with respect to their entire pay. But in that case, the manager is in pretty much the same position as the owners of the company, so why wouldn't he start his own company?

Most likely, the manager is risk-averse and wants some way to avoid bearing the uncontrollable risk of the firm, which means passing it on to the owners of the company. How do we escape from this dilemma?

MEASURING EFFORT AND PERFORMANCE

To the extent that managerial effort can be measured indirectly, the opportunities for managers to shirk can be minimized. Both input and output can be measured.

A typical input measure would be the number of hours the manager spends on the job. Other input measures would include the cost of items used in the production process. For our SkiTrails manager, such input measures could include the number of hours spent at the resort, the cost of snow-making, expenditures on advertising, and so on. The assumption is that the quality of whatever input is being measured is constant and that there is a recognizable relationship between input and output. From an accounting perspective, organizing the firm into cost centers and evaluating managers on the basis of costs alone is essentially an input-based monitoring system.

For managers, though, output measures are more likely to be used than input measures. These measures are not direct measures of effort but, instead, are what are called instrumental measures. They either measure something that is thought to be closely related to effort or compare outputs to inputs. Historically, such measures have included net income, profit margins, return on assets and return on equity (both measures that compare outputs to inputs), and growth in earnings and sales. In terms of maximizing the wealth of the existing owners of the company, the company's stock price is also assumed to be related to these measures. So, increasingly, more and more companies are using the stock price itself or some compensation scheme that ties rewards to the stock price to finesse the ever-present problem of measuring effort. Still, the problem of separating the contributions management makes to performance from factors that are not under management control (luck, noise) remains. How do we get out of this box?

Measures of relative performance may be one answer. Owners can measure managerial performance relative to the performance of other firms in the industry or some other benchmark. For example, managerial performance can be benchmarked against such industrywide financial ratios as profit margins, return on assets, return on shareholders' equity, and rates of growth in sales and net income. As we will discover, many companies do use such relative performance measures and measure performance against "peer groups."

With respect to the stock price, managerial performance can be evaluated by adjusting the change in the company's stock price for what happened to the market in general—all companies—during the same period. Suppose the per share price of XYZ Corporation fell by 8 percent over the year. Was the decline in the share price due to poor management or to factors beyond the control of management, such as an economywide recession? Some insights into this question can be gained by looking at what happened to a broad-based market index such as the Standard & Poor's 500. If the index fell by 20 percent, perhaps the managers of XYZ Corporation should be paid a substantial bonus because they were able to guide the company through the recession far better than the managers of other companies. However, if the index rose by 20 percent during the period, a different story emerges.

COMMON PAY AND PERFORMANCE SCHEMES

In the United States, senior managers' pay typically has three components: a fixed or base salary, a short-term or annual bonus payment, and a long-term bonus or performance payment. Both the short-term and long-term bonus payments are tied to performance measures, with the long-term bonus often taking the form of stock options. In 1996, the median CEO pay, inclusive of all forms of compensation, was $3.2 million in mining and manufacturing, $4.6 million in financial services, and, $1.5 million in utilities.[1]

For U.S. CEOs, the fixed base cash salary represents between 20 and 40 percent of total compensation, with the fixed salary percentage being lowest among large manufacturing firms and financial services companies (a category that includes investment banks) and highest among utilities. Furthermore, the CEO's base salary as a percentage of total compensation has been dropping since 1990. However, one explanation for the reduction in fixed salaries as a percentage of compensation may be a 1993 change in the U.S. tax code that prohibited firms from deducting as business expenses nonperformance pay over $1 million to executives. Consequently, any compensation in excess of $1 million is likely to be disguised in one form or another as incentive-based pay.

Base Salary Examples

Base salaries for senior managers are set by the compensation committee of the board of directors. At Genuine Parts Company (GPS), the compensation committee sets the base salary of the CEO based on (1) the CEO's base salary the previous year, (2) increases in the cost of living, (3) increased responsibilities, (4) compensation of CEOs in the company's Peer Index, and (5) the CEO's past performance. The Peer Index for GPS is a company-constructed index of firms in similar lines of business; it includes firms in the automotive parts, industrial parts, office products, and electrical materials industries. Base compensation for other executive officers of GPS is then set by the CEO and the compensation committee using the same criteria.

The compensation committee of First Virginia Banks sets the base salary of executives as a function of (1) the degree of responsibility the officer has and the officer's experience and service and (2) the compensation levels of corresponding positions at other banking companies that make up what First Virginia calls a local peer group. The committee uses the median salaries of the local peer group as a target. This procedure produced a base salary of $600,000 for the CEO in 1999, which was 101.5 percent of median salaries for his counterparts.

Note, though, that using peer-group averages may tend to ratchet up everyone's pay over time. This outcome occurs because of a tendency to raise the pay of everyone who is below the average to the average, causing the average to move up (unless, of course, everyone is above average, as in Lake Wobegon).

Short-Term Incentive Plans

Short-term (annual) incentive pay plans tie a portion of managerial pay to the performance of the company over the past year; hence the term *annual incentive plans*. These plans consist of performance measures, individual and group standards or goals, and a system for relating managerial pay to the goals. In the 1990s, these plans made up about 20 percent of CEOs' total pay.

Performance measures for short-term incentive plans almost always include one or more financial statement metrics. Typically, some measure of accounting income is used, such as earnings before interest and taxes (EBIT), net income before taxes, net income after taxes, and/or earnings per share. In addition to levels of income, rates of return on assets, stockholders' equity, or sales may also be used. Occasionally, rates of growth in sales or income may be included as well.

Individual and group performance is measured against standards. These standards may be the previous year's actual performance, a budget, or some absolute standard that remains the same from one year to the next. The typical plan sets a minimum standard that must be reached before any bonus is paid, and also sets a cap on the maximum bonus that will be paid regardless of how well the manager performs.

For example, the manager's performance may be measured against last year's net income after taxes. The minimum or threshold level may be achieving at least the same net income as in the previous year. Once this threshold is reached, an increasing bonus is paid up to, say, a 20 percent increase in net income over the previous year. Increases in net income beyond 20 percent, however, do not generate additional payments. If a budget is used, the manager's performance is measured against the budget and not the prior year's performance. An example of an absolute standard would be earning a return on assets of, say, at least 10 percent.

Group incentive pay plans create a pool of dollars conditional on group performance that are distributed to the individual managers within the group in accordance with some scheme. Individual managerial performance may affect the way the group pool of dollars is ultimately divided among the managers.

Short-Term Incentive Examples

In 2001, First Virginia Banks had a short-term incentive program that granted bonuses to executive officers and the CEO if First Virginia achieved a return on total average assets (ROA) of at least 1 percent. An ROA of 1 percent was used because the compensation committee believed that ROA is the most important single factor in measuring the performance of a banking company, and that a 1 percent ROA is the minimum for a good-performing banking company.

First Virginia awarded a bonus of up to 50 percent of an executive's salary if the bank achieved an ROA equivalent to 80 percent or more of the ROA target amount for the year. For the CEO, First Virginia would also have to achieve 80 percent of the targeted amounts for return on equity, asset quality as determined by the ratio of nonperforming loans to total assets, and capital strength based on the average equity-to-asset ratio and the Tier 1 risk-based capital ratio. Also, a bonus was paid based on the degree to which First Virginia's earnings, asset quality, and capital ratios exceeded the average for other major banking companies in the Southeast. Note again that this latter bonus was tied to relative and not absolute performance, as performance was measured against competitors.

In 1999, Genuine Parts Company (GPC) had a short-term incentive plan that provided approximately 48 percent of its executives' total annual compensation but could rise as high as 62 percent. GPC's annual incentive plan was based on goals set by the company. A projected pretax return expressed as a percentage of shareholders' equity at the beginning of the year—a budget-based performance standard—was deemed the most important measure, but GPC also set sales targets and return on assets targets. In 1999, the CEO of GPC earned an annual bonus equal to 61 percent of his total annual compensation. The annual bonus was determined 90 percent by meeting the return on equity goal, 5 percent by meeting the sales goal, and 5 percent by meeting the return on assets goal.

Problems with Short-Term Incentive Plans

Short-term incentive plans do not always align the interests of managers with those of the public shareholders. Problems arise because accounting measures are used, because performance standards can be manipulated, and because managers can game the system by transferring effort from one period to another.

Problems with Accounting Measures

The use of accounting measures such as net income, earnings per share, and return on assets or equity assumes that these measures are highly correlated with stock prices. They often are, but not in quite the way that is often supposed, especially because they can be manipulated. Stock prices are correlated with future earnings, not past earnings—there is a lead-lag correlation, with stock prices predicting future earnings.

One important fact to remember about accounting-based

performance measures is that they look backward, not forward. Net income, for example, measures the difference between past revenues and past expenses. Therefore, managers can manipulate net income by reducing expenditures on such things as advertising, research and development, and employee training programs in order to "earn" higher bonuses under a short-term accounting-based incentive scheme. But, the consequences of such actions are likely to be reduced cash inflows and earnings in the future, which will be bad for the stock price because the stock price is determined by expectations of future cash flows.

Problems with Budgets

A second important fact to remember about accounting profits is that managers can manipulate them to move profits from one accounting period to the next. Examples would include the choice of depreciation schedules for assets, accruals of expenses, and booking of revenues. Indeed, managers commonly use discretionary accounting rules to smooth earnings from one year to the next in order to avoid reporting large one-time gains or losses in income. Thus, managers can game bonus plans through manipulating accounting earnings.

Another major problem with short-term bonus plan performance standards is that managers are usually involved in setting the standards, especially if the standard is a consensus budget. Hence, managers can influence the standards that are set and, therefore, performance outcomes. Knowing that their pay will be affected by how they perform relative to a budget, managers may be inclined to underestimate budgeted revenues and overestimate budgeted expenses.

Absolute performance standards such as a 10 percent return on equity are less susceptible to such gaming, but only if the managers do not exert influence over the standard. A classic example of managers gaming the bonus system by setting their own absolute performance standard is a Deutsche Bank stock option plan in the early 1990s. Deutsche Bank managers implemented a pay scheme that would give them bonuses if the return on Deutsche Bank common stock merely equaled the return on default-free German government bonds!

Potential Gaming Behavior

Finally, the thresholds and caps on short-term plans can also induce managerial gaming. Suppose a manager faces the following incentive plan: She receives a bonus of 20 percent of base salary if net income for the year is greater than $100 million, and the bonus rises to 25 percent if net income is $150 million. No additional bonus is paid if net income exceeds $150 million. If the likelihood that net income for the year will reach $100 million is nil, she has no incentive to exert additional effort for that year and every incentive to incur expenses this year and push revenue into next year. She faces the same incentive if net income is likely to be above $150 million. She receives no additional bonus this year for income over $150 million, so, again, why not book expenses this year and delay sales until next year?

Okay, so if there are all these problems with short-term incentive plans based on accounting income and related accounting measures, why are the plans so common? The answer is that accounting numbers are verifiable and are calculated according to a set of generally accepted rules. Managers know the rules and can predict the effects of their behavior on their pay. This predictability means that managers can focus their attention on those metrics that those who design the plans believe are important for maximizing shareholder wealth and not worry about after-the-fact reinterpretations of performance being used to change the rules of the game.

In summary, the problems of short-term incentive plans can be mitigated if multiple performance measures that are more difficult for managers to game than a single metric are used, if standards are set externally, and if absolute standards are used instead of budgets or comparisons to prior year performance. Still, these plans may result in managers making short-term decisions that are not in the best interests of the shareholders, so, long-term incentive plans are also used to compensate managers.

Long-Term Incentive Plans

Long-term incentive plans tie a portion of managerial pay to some long-term performance measure. The measure(s) can be the same accounting-based measures described earlier or the stock price of the company. When accounting measures are used, performance is evaluated over more than one year. Typically, the manager must remain with the firm for a specified length of time in order to receive bonuses earned under long-term incentive plans. The bonuses may be paid in cash, restricted stock, or stock options. Restricted stock is a grant of shares in the company that may not be sold or disposed of prior to a future date and that may be forfeited if the manager leaves before the end of the restricted period.

Increasingly, stock options are the preferred form of payment in the United States, with over 30 percent of CEO compensation coming in the form of stock options in all industries except utilities in the mid-1990s. The typical stock option traded in financial markets is a financial contract that gives the owner the right but not the obligation to buy or sell stock at a specified price, called the strike or exercise price, through a specified period of time, called the option's expiration date. A call option is the right to buy stock; a put option is the right to sell the stock at the strike price.

The value of the option can be calculated with the Black-

Scholes option pricing model. For a detailed description of this model, you should consult a book on investments. For our purposes, the two important determinants of an option's value are the difference between the strike price and the market price of the stock and the volatility of the underlying stock. For a call option (which is what managers receive), the option becomes more valuable as the market price of the stock rises above the strike price. So, when a manager receives options to buy common stock in her company at, say, $40 a share, the options increase in value as the company's stock price rises above $40 a share. Should the stock price fall to $20 a share, the options would be worthless.

The other important determinant is the volatility of the stock price. The more volatile the stock price, the more valuable the option. Look at it this way: Why would anyone buy an option on a stock selling for, say, $60 a share today if they knew that the price of the stock would always be $60? Contrast this situation with one in which the stock price could be $100 or $10 a year from today. Under these circumstances an option to buy at $60 would be worth money. If the stock rises to $100, exercise the option and make $40; if it falls to $10, let the option expire. And contrast this situation to one in which the stock price could be $500 or $5 a year from today. Now the option to buy the stock is worth even more than when the stock price could range between $10 and $100 a share.

The options given to managers under long-term incentive programs usually have some restrictions attached to them. Most often, the options cannot be exercised immediately but must be held for a specified number of years—a process called vesting. Furthermore, the options cannot be sold, and if the manager leaves the firm before the vesting period, the options are voided. Other conditions can also be placed on the stock option grants, such as mandating that the stock price must reach a certain level before the options are given to the manager.

Examples of Long-Term Incentive Plans

GPC's restricted stock plan is typical of many such plans. During 1999, GPC agreed to make future grants of restricted stock based upon increases in the company's stock price and the achievement of certain earnings per share targets between 1999 and 2003. GPC also has a stock option plan. In 2000, GPC granted options to purchase 2,408,000 shares of common stock at fair market value (set as the market price on the granting date) to 357 employees.

First Virginia granted options covering a total of 220,500 shares of First Virginia stock to executives in 2000. These options vested over a five-year period in equal installments.

Brush Wellman had a long-term incentive plan in effect from 1995 through 1999 that granted restricted stock awards based on management objectives measured over three years. The awards were based on achieving a target level of return on invested capital. The target was not met, and the CEO forfeited the 19,639 performance restricted shares that had been granted him in 1996.

In 1998, Brush Wellman set up a new restricted stock performance award with objectives based solely on stock price appreciation between 1998 and 2000. Under this plan, the CEO was granted 11,606 performance restricted shares, which would be forfeited—as happened under the 1995 plan—if the stock price goal was not met.

Problems with Stock Option and Restricted Stock Plans

The theory behind granting managers stock options is that those who receive stock options will make decisions that lead to share price appreciation because the value of the stock option is tied to the share price. And at first glance, stock options appear to have no drawbacks associated with them. However, problems do exist, and many of them have come to light with the decline in stock prices in 2000 and 2001, the collapse of many "new-economy" stocks, and the failure of telecommunications companies and Enron.

Let's start with cash dividends. Executives who hold stock options do not receive cash dividends. Therefore, these executives may be inclined to retain earnings rather than return them to the public shareholders. Recall from our discussion of the stock price valuation model that reinvested earnings are the fundamental cause of growth in stock prices, and it is this growth—capital gains—that is captured by managers who hold options.

Alternatively, managers may prefer to repurchase the company's stock rather than distribute the cash to shareholders as cash dividends. If there are fewer shares outstanding, per share earnings will increase, leading to an increase in the per share stock price. Empirical evidence supporting reduced cash dividend payouts and increased share repurchases by managers whose compensation is strongly tied to stock options does exist.[2]

Another potential problem with stock options and restricted stock is that managers may take on very risky investments if the stock price has fallen or if the stock price goals under a restricted stock plan appear unlikely to be met. As we noted earlier in this chapter, a major determinant of the value of stock options is the volatility of the underlying stock. An increase in stock price volatility causes an increase in the value of the option. And the way to increase stock price volatility is to make more risky investments. However, while this is a valid theoretical argument, we suspect that the losses a manager would incur if the firm failed more than outweigh the potential gains from taking on risky negative net present value investments just to increase the value of the option.

Reported Earnings and Paying Managers with Stock or Stock Options

The most visible problems with using options to compensate managers that have surfaced involve earnings and earnings manipulation. Consider this question: Should the value of the options granted management be recorded as an expense—in the same way that salaries are an expense—and thereby result in a lowered net income and earnings per share? Put it a bit differently: Does the failure to deduct the value of the options given management understate expenses and overstate net income? And, whether it does or doesn't overstate net income, does it affect the way investors value the company's common stock?

The argument for recording options and restricted stock as an expense is that these grants, if exercised or vested, will cause the claims of existing shareholders on the assets, cash flows, and earnings of the company to be diluted. For example, take two companies that are identical with regard to everything except how they pay their CEO. The data are given in Figure 8-1. Each company has 10 million shares of stock outstanding with a share price of $200 a share, for a total market value of $2 billion. A public shareholder, JQP, who owns 1 million shares owns 10 percent of the company and is entitled to 10 percent of any dividends and earnings. Before paying and accounting for the CEO's compensation, the earnings and cash flows available to the shareholders of both companies are $300 million.

Now, Company A pays its CEO $10 million, resulting in net income of $290 million being reported on the company's income statement. The $10 million salary paid to the CEO leaves the company, so the market value of the company falls to $1.99 billion. The company can either retain the $290 million in earnings or distribute them as cash dividends. In either case, our public investor has a claim on 10 percent of

FIGURE 8-1   THE EFFECTS OF PAYING MANAGERS IN STOCK ON THE MARKET VALUE, REPORTED EARNINGS, AND CASH FLOWS OF A COMPANY

	Company A	Company Z
Market value	$2,000,000,000	$2,000,000,000
Outstanding shares of stock	10,000,000 shares	10,000,000 shares
Per share price	$200.00	$200.00
Cash flow before CEO pay	$100,000,000	$100,000,000
CEO salary	$10,000,000	$0
Cash flow after CEO salary	$290,000,000	$300,000,000
Net income after CEO salary	**$290,000,000**	**$300,000,000**
Grant of 50,251.26 shares worth $10,000,000 to CEO		Equal to 0.5% of $2,000,000,000 and 0.5% of new total of outstanding shares, which must be 10,050,251.26
Market value of the company after CEO pay	$1,990,000,000	$2,000,000,000
Number of shares outstanding	10,000,000	10,050,251.6
Per share market value	$199.00	$199.00
Market value of 10,000,000 shares held by JQP	**$199,000,000**	**$199,000,000**

the earnings or dividends, for a total claim of $29,000,000, and, the value of his holdings would be $199 million.

In contrast, Company Z pays its CEO in restricted stock. So, at the end of the year, the CEO receives a conditional stock grant worth $10 million. But, how much stock should she receive? Well, the total market value of the company will still be $2 billion because no cash has left the company to pay the CEO. Instead, the CEO will be given stock with a market value equal to $10 million. Whatever the number of shares given the CEO, they must represent 0.5 percent of the new number of shares outstanding after the CEO has received these shares. The old public shareholders will now own only 99.5 percent of the post-stock award number of shares. Thus, the new total number of shares outstanding must be 10,000,000 shares divided by 0.995, or 10,050,251.6, and the CEO must receive 50,251.6 shares if she is to own 0.5 percent of the company.

Now we can continue our story. Look at the net income that would have been reported had the CEO been paid with a restricted stock grant. The net income would have been $300 million, as compared to $290 million if a pure salary compensation scheme had been used. It looks as if the earnings are higher under the stock compensation plan. But, in reality, JQP, our public investor, finds himself in exactly the same position under either plan. In both cases he ends up with $199 million, despite the fact that Company Z reported higher earnings. What happened?

Well, in the case of Company Z, the CEO was given potential ownership in the company for "free." She did not have to invest any cash. So, instead of being divvied up among 10,000,000 shares, the $300 million in earnings must now be divvied up among 10,050,251.6 shares. Each old shareholder gets a smaller percentage of the pie. This is called dilution of shareholders' equity. So, yes, compensating managers with restricted stock and with stock options (which are treated similarly with respect to expenses and net income) is, effectively, a cost that isn't presently recognized on the income statements of publicly held corporations.

But we still haven't answered the question of whether investors are fooled by this accounting convention. Will the stock of Company Z have a higher price than that of Company A because of the apparent higher earnings? Not in efficient markets.

Abusive Manipulation of Earnings

More of a problem than whether stock options are recorded as an expense and a reduction in net income is what we will call abusive earnings manipulations—legal and illegal.

You are the CEO of NewEconomyTech, otherwise known as NETECH. Your pay is tied to the stock price of NETECH, and you also hold a substantial number of options on NETECH stock. You firmly believe that NETECH's stock price is tied to its reported earnings, and especially to the rate of growth in earnings. Furthermore, your stock has been touted by many Wall Street analysts, who have predicted double-digit earnings growth for NETECH. These analysts meet with you quarterly and ask for your assessment of whether NETECH will meet its earnings targets (forecasts). Your assessments are called "earnings guidance" in Wall Street jargon, and coming in under these targets can cause NETECH's stock price to tank. So, what do you do?

Well, as long as things are going well for NETECH, you don't have a problem. But, sooner or later, NETECH will no longer be able to grow at 60 percent a year without becoming larger than the entire world's economy. So, as NETECH's growth slows down, you look for ways to conceal this through the use of aggressive accounting conventions. Eventually, you and your auditors, who are also your management consultants, run out of legal aggressive accounting conventions, and you find yourself on the edge of legality with respect to booking revenues, recognizing expenses, and reporting the company's debt obligations. Do you step over the line? Does your auditor help you step over the line in order to keep your consulting business? Or, do you "fess up," tell the analysts that earnings will not come anywhere near what they forecasted, and take the hit on the stock price?

For someone who wants a corporate governance system that makes it possible for firms to finance investments as cheaply as possible (to create jobs and income) and to allocate capital efficiently, abusive manipulations of earnings, often achieved at the expense of the long-run health of the firm and, more importantly, the economy, are not what is wanted. So, how do you prevent this?

One way is to simply prohibit pay schemes such as stock

options so as to remove the temptations of managers to manipulate earnings. But then the benefits of these schemes are also lost. Another way is to reform the rules and institutions for auditing the books of publicly held corporations, including the responsibilities and legal accountability of managers and auditors. We return to these questions in the closing chapter.

EVA®: A VERY POPULAR COMPENSATION PLAN AND CORPORATE GOVERNANCE METRIC

EVA® or some variation of it is widely used among U.S. corporations. For example, Georgia-Pacific says in its 2000 Annual Review, "We use EVA® metrics . . . to improve our understanding of risk and return tradeoffs." EVA is also used by investment bankers, including Goldman Sachs and Credit Suisse First Boston, for valuing companies around the world. Furthermore, according to Stern Stewart, major institutional investors use EVA to select companies to include in investment portfolios. And the California Public Employee Retirement System uses EVA to identify companies that need corporate governance reforms. So what is it?

EVA stands for Economic Value Added and is a trademarked product of Stern Stewart & Company. Although other similar products exist, we use EVA as a vehicle for explaining how corporate boards are trying to connect managerial pay to performance and align the interests of managers with those of public shareholders. Also, EVA has come under extensive scrutiny by financial economists, so there is an ever-growing body of empirical work evaluating its effectiveness.

Earlier in the book, we defined NPV as the difference between the present value of the expected after-tax cash flows from an investment project and the present value of the cash outflows invested in the project, both discounted at the project's cost of capital. The greater the NPV, the better the project with respect to creating shareholder wealth and increasing the stock price. We also showed the connection between a project's NPV and its market-to-book ratio: The greater the NPV, the greater the market-to-book ratio. EVA is simply a way of measuring whether managers have been able to undertake positive NPV projects and earn a return for the shareholders that is greater than the investors' required rate of return on the stock.

A manager adds economic value when she can earn a return over and above the company's cost of capital. The result will be a company that has a market value greater than its book value. We draw extensively on an explanation of EVA put forth by G. Bennett Stewart, III, a member of Stern Stewart and an advocate of EVA.[3]

A STYLIZED EVA EXAMPLE

Consider an all-equity company, Value-Gain, with a market value (MV) of $900 million and a book value (BV) of $600 million. Book value is the dollar value of its shareholders' equity. Figure 8-2 contains stylized financial statements for Value-Gain. Value-Gain has 10 million shares of common stock outstanding, so its book value per share is $60 and its market value per share is $90. The investors' required rate of return on Value-Gain stock is 10 percent.

The difference between the market value and the book value is $300 million; under EVA, this is called the market value added (MVA). MVA corresponds to NPV for a single investment for which the present value of the cash inflows would be $900 million, the present value of the cash outflows would be $600 million, and the NPV would be $300 million.

Figure 8-2   Value-Gain Market and Financial Data
(All dollar amounts except per share data in
millions)

Market Value Data

Market value of company (MV)	$900.0
Investors' required return on common stock k	0.10

Balance Sheet Data

Total assets	$600.0
Stockholders' equity and book value (BV) 10 million shares of common stock outstanding. Book value per share is $60	$600.0

Income Statement Data

Net income	$90.0
Less capital charge of 10 percent of $600.0 million	$60.0
EVA	$30.0

Per Share Data

Market value per share	$90.00
Book value per share	$60.00
Earnings per share	$9.00
Dividends per share	$9.00

$$\text{MVA} = \text{MV} - \text{BV} = \$900 - \$600 = \$300$$
$$\text{EVA} = \text{NI} - k(\text{NI}) = \$90 - 0.10(\$90) = \$30$$
$$\text{MVA} = \text{EVA}/k = \$30/0.10 = \$300$$

Recall that back in Chapter 5 we calculated the present value of Snail Fish as $427,181, subtracted from this amount its cost of $300,000, and said that Snail Fish has a NPV of $127,181. We then said that this positive NPV meant that the returns that Lamprey Products shareholders could earn on Snail Fish were greater than both the 14 percent cost of capital for the project and the returns that Lamprey Products's shareholders could earn on the $300,000 anywhere else. Well, in the Snail Fish example, the MVA for the Snail Fish investment is its $127,181 NPV, with $300,000 being the book value for Snail Fish and $427,181 being its market value. In other words, the managements of Lamprey Products and Value-Gain are creating value for shareholders by earning returns in excess of investors' required rates of return—the company's cost of capital.

To continue, suppose that the $900 million market value ($90 a share) of Value-Gain came from investors' expectations that this company would generate after-tax net income in cash of $90 million a year ($9 a share) for ever and ever and that all earnings would be paid out as cash dividends ($9). Given the investors' required rate of return k on this company of 10 percent, the market value of the equity of one share of stock would be $90, calculated as:

$$P_0 = \frac{D_1}{k-g} = \frac{\$9}{0.10-0} = \$90$$

The market value of the company, of course, is $90 per share times 10 million shares, or $900 million.

Now, think about the $90 million of net income (NI) in Figure 8-2 that is reported each year on the company's income statement. Suppose we make one more adjustment to net income and call it the cost of equity capital (or equity capital financing charge), which is simply our investors' required rate of return on the common stock. This charge should be 10 percent of the capital that the shareholders have provided to management to generate the earnings. The capital for our all-equity firm, shareholders' equity, is $600 million and the equity capital financing charge is $60 million.

So, let's subtract the equity capital financing charge of $60 million from the $90 million net income. We end up with $30 million. This $30 million is called EVA, or the economic value added by management. When we capitalize this $30 million annual EVA at the 10 percent cost of equity capital, we have $300 million, an amount that is exactly equal to the MVA, the difference between market value and book value.

Relating the EVA framework to our presentation on investment analysis, then, the market value MV of a company is the analog of the present value of an investment project. The book value BV of a company is the analog of the cash outflows needed to make that investment. And the EVA is the value of the cash flows the project earns over and above its cost of capital, discounted at the project's cost of capital.

Using EVA to Set Compensation

Okay, what does this mean for a management compensation scheme that aligns the interests of managers with those of shareholders? Well, again to keep it simple, executive short-term incentive plan bonuses can be tied to EVA. The compensation committee calculates the company's cost of equity capital k and applies it to the assets (shareholders' equity) under the control of the manager. Then the accounting net income of the company or division under the control of the manager is reduced by this equity capital financing charge. The annual bonus then becomes a function of the remainder, called EVA. Positive EVAs are good news for the manager's bonus; negative EVAs are bad news—not only for bonuses but for the likelihood that the division will remain part of the company.

A specific example of how EVA has been implemented is the case of SPX, a large U.S. auto parts and industrial company. SPX was an underperformer in the 1990s in terms of both profitability and share price. With the arrival of a new CEO in 1995, SPX adopted an EVA bonus plan for its senior managers, and eventually for 4,700 other managers. The stock price of SPX subsequently rose from $16 to $180 a share—an outcome that the company attributed to the mind-set created by the EVA plan's focus on value added. SPX also experienced improvements in asset efficiency, led by a reduction in inventories. The EVA plan, by focusing managerial attention on the capital costs of holding inventory and, more important, tying managerial bonuses to earnings in excess of capital costs, motivated managers to monitor and reduce inventories, which translated into a reduction in the amount of capital (book value) needed to support a given level of net income.

Our description of EVA is very basic. Many modifications are made to fit the plan to each company's special needs and circumstances. For detailed descriptions of EVA, contact Stern Stewart Management Services.

THE EVIDENCE ABOUT PAY AND PERFORMANCE

Okay, let's ask the really important question: What is the evidence concerning managerial pay and performance? Well, it's mixed.

Some early studies by financial economists found that the stock prices of companies that announced stock-based compensation plans went up on the announcement day, indicating that investors saw such plans as good news. But these are one-time events, and so the question becomes whether any additional investor benefits were forthcoming.

What about the relationship between market value and book value, a relationship that is at the core of EVA? Well, here again the findings are mixed. There is some evidence that companies in which managers own more stock exhibit higher market-to-book ratios than companies in which managers own less stock. Furthermore, some studies show that market-to-book ratios are also positively related to the percentage of executive compensation that is tied to stock options and restricted stock. But what is the cause and effect? Does stock-based compensation for managers lead to higher market-to-book ratios, or do managers of companies with high market-to-book ratios demand stock-based compensation and managers of mature companies with low market-to-book ratios simply ask for other forms of compensation? We don't really know.

What we do know is that whatever connection exists between pay and stock prices or shareholder returns is explained by annual and long-term incentive compensation, not by the base or fixed salary. We also know that that executive pay is most sensitive to performance in the manufacturing and financial industries and least sensitive among public utilities. And we have evidence that suggests that executive pay is more sensitive to performance in smaller than in larger firms. Finally, it seems that pay became more sensitive to stock price performance in the latter half of the 1990s. But is this merely a statistical artifact, given that equity prices rose through the 1990s, or is there really a cause-and-effect relationship? We are about to find out.

PAY AND PERFORMANCE IN 2000

In March 2000, the NASDAQ peaked at a little over 5000; in June 2001, it hovered at around 2000, for a loss of over 50 percent. Over the same period, the S&P 500 index fell from over 1500 to 1200, for a decline of 20 percent. During this same period, corporate profits fell, and many financial and economic observers worried that we either were in or were about to enter a recession. So, what happened to executive compensation, and especially to performance-based compensation involving stock options?

Well, in absolute terms, executive compensation continued to increase. Cash compensation for CEOs of large U.S.

companies increased by 10 percent in 2000, compared to 5.2 percent in 1999 and 5.2 percent in 1998.[4] With stock prices off by 20 to 50 percent, is this what is meant by "pay for performance"?

Take a look at Figure 8-3. Panel A contains information about CEO compensation in 2000 for forty-five large industrial and basic material companies whose stock underperformed industry peers. Absolute one-year shareholder returns are also included in the figure, and only five of the companies showed shareholder gains and not losses. The CEOs of thirty of these companies (67 percent) saw their salary and bonus increase over 1999.

Panel B contains comparable data for the companies whose one-year stock price performance was better than that of their industry peers. Here, as expected, twenty-one of the twenty-eight CEOs were awarded increases in salary and bonuses. Interestingly, though, six of the eight CEOs who saw a reduction in compensation led companies whose absolute shareholder returns were negative.

Given the limited sample size, both in numbers and in years, one must be very careful about generalizations. However, the early returns from 2001 suggest that executive pay did fall in response to the declining fortunes of many companies. A survey of 100 companies conducted by William M. Mercer, Inc., for the *Wall Street Journal* found that salaries and bonuses of CEOs dropped by 2.9 percent to $1.24 million in the face of a 13 percent drop in profits.[5]

However, evidence to the contrary also exists. There were some very-high-profile cases in 2001. For example, Richard McGinn, a former CEO of Lucent Technologies, was granted $12.5 million in severance pay when he was ousted in October 2000 after Lucent missed financial targets and the SEC began to look into potential accounting irregularities. Former Enron CEO Kenneth Lay sold $70.1 million of stock back to Enron between February and October 2001. Then, in

FIGURE 8-3   CEO COMPENSATION IN 2000

A. CEO Compensation in Large Industrial and Basic Material Companies Whose Stock Underperformed Industry Peers

Company	2000 Salary and Bonus (000)	Percent Change from 1999 in Salary and Bonus	1-Year Shareholder Return	Shareholder Return Compared to Industry Peers, %
Litton	1,421.0	38.5	− 28.1	− 5,686.6
CSX	1,100.0	0.0	− 13.0	− 3,372.8
UPS	1,532.4	2.4	− 13.8	− 3,183.2
Avery Dennison	1,808.4	7.6	− 23.3	− 2,105.8
Norfolk Southern	1,360.4	43.2	− 31.6	− 488.8
Airborne	650.0	7.6	− 54.7	− 386.7
Ikon	1,537.8	2.5	− 63.6	− 375.3
Pittson	961.5	− 16.4	− 9.2	− 352.3
DuPont	$2,740.0	− 2.1%	− 24.4%	− 314.4
Textron	2,937.5	22.4	− 37.8	− 305.1
Pentair	1,089.9	22.1	− 35.9	− 305.0
Fluor	1,050.0	− 44.7	− 9.6	− 229.4
Roadway Express	825.8	5.9	− 1.5	− 201.5
Dover	2,170.0	11.3	− 9.6	− 160.8
Illinois Tool Works	2,209.5	8.0	− 10.7	− 156.0
Rockwell International	2,200.0	− 12.9	− 17.5	− 144.0
Parker-Hannifin	1,889.2	11.9	− 24.1	− 142.3
National Service	850.0	− 52.4	− 34.1	− 138.3
Freeport-Mason	4,125.0	10.0	− 58.1	− 122.7
Freeport-McMoRan	4,125.0	10.0	− 58.1	− 122.7
Texas Industries	1,186.2	37.8	− 20.5	− 122.7
Owens-Illinois	1,200.8	6.7	− 77.3	− 112.4
Georgia-Pacific	3,000.0	− 4.8	− 37.8	− 107.7

FIGURE 8-3   (Continued).

Company	2000 Salary and Bonus (000)	Percent Change from 1999 in Salary and Bonus	1-Year Shareholder Return	Shareholder Return Compared to Industry Peers, %
Mead	1,350.8	2.9	− 26.0	− 107.6
Tyco International	4,150.0	− 8.8	0.6	− 97.5
Briggs & Stratton	1,388,1	14.8	− 39.1	− 84.7
Crown Cork and Seal	981.6	− 35.6	− 62.7	− 77.0
U.S. Ind.	750.0	− 46.7	− 35.8	− 54.8
Avnet	1,265.0	35.7	27.3	− 51.7
Emerson Electric	7,400.0	76.2	8.3	− 51.6
Timken	1,128.8	32.8	− 22.7	− 50.8
Weyerhaeuser	2,900.0	16.6	− 26.9	− 48.8
First Data	1,786.0	13.4	7.0	− 43.6
Cooper Ind.	1,842.5	16.5	18.7	− 39.5
FedEx	2,141.8	0.9	− 32.2	− 39.0
Goodrich (B.F.)	2,275.9	23.2	36.5	− 36.7
General Electric	16,700.0	25.3	− 6.1	− 33.9
Louisiana-Pacific	750.0	− 45.3	− 23.8	− 31.2
Electronic Data Systems	4,912.8	− 4.3	− 13.2	− 30.5
General Dynamics	2,700.0	13.1	50.4	− 12.5
Jacobs Engineering	1,063.1	− 14.1	− 29.1	− 12.3
Navistar	975.0	− 6.5	− 21.3	− 10.8
CNF	991.4	− 35.9	− 0.4	− 5.9
Boise Cascade	995.4	− 35.0	− 15.3	15.6
Grainger (W.W.)	1,203.3	31.6	− 22.4	31.4
Number positive		30	7	2
Number negative		15	38	43

(continues on p. 146)

Figure 8-3   (Continued).

B. CEO Compensation in Large Industrial and Basic Material Companies Whose Stock Outperformed Industry Peers

Company	2000 Salary and Bonus (000)	Percent Change from 1999 in Salary and Bonus	1-Year Shareholder Return	Shareholder Return Compared to Industry Peers, %
Lubrizol	1,227.0	−19.8	−12.9	1.0
PPG Ind.	1,690.0	−0.6	−22.7	5.5
International Paper	2,064.4	8.1	−25.2	10.8
Lockheed Martin	3,792.6	201.5	58.3	12.0
Boeing	4,672.5	9.7	61.3	50.0
Tecumseh Products	524.8	−25.0	−4.9	69.9
Commercial Metals	1,080.0	18.7	−7.2	76.0
Applera	2,177.5	−9.2	176.4	81.2
Toro	1,211.1	−4.6	−1.0	84.5
Westavo	1,375.0	57.1	−1.2	93.2
Worthington Ind.	964.0	4.0	−1.2	95.3
Willamette Industries	1,033.3	19.2	3.5	119.2
Eastman Chemical	2,131.0	41.4	6.4	138.5
Crane	1,566.4	23.0	45.2	140.3
Corning	2,448.3	7.8	23.4	141.6
Ball	1,709.4	−2.2	19.7	155.7
Olin	1,172.8	40.0	16.9	163.0
Stanley Works	2,800.0	20.4	7.3	181.4
Air Products	$2,184.5	58.8	25.6	201.3
Cabot	1,425.0	26.7	35.8	266.0
Paccar	1,070.0	−39.4	16.1	276.9
Automatic Data Processing	1,247.5	9.1	22.6	298.4
ITT	2,575.0	1.6	18.5	379.2
United Technologies	3,600.0	5.9	22.5	581.9
Minn. Mining & Mfg.	3,244.0	17.1	26.1	654.4

FIGURE 8-3   (*Continued*).

Company	2000 Salary and Bonus (000)	Percent Change from 1999 in Salary and Bonus	1-Year Shareholder Return	Shareholder Return Compared to Industry Peers, %
Donnelley	1,747.3	4.3	13.2	816.3
FMC	2,367.2	88.6	25.1	1,301.4
Union Pacific	3,362.5	16.5	18.5	1,463.6
Number positive		21	20	28
Number negative		7	8	0

Source: "The Boss's Pay," *Wall Street Journal*, April 12, 2001, pp. R12–R15.

mid-October, Enron reported very large losses attributable to partnerships run by Enron executives. And in January 2002, Kmart directors dismissed Charles Conaway as chairman five days before Kmart filed for bankruptcy. However, the directors left him in charge of the company as CEO, paid him a bonus of $6.6 million, and forgave a loan of $5 million that the company had made to him for as long as he worked for the company.[6]

Critics further point to the frequency with which managerial stock options that were "under water" were repriced as stock prices fell. By under water, we mean that the exercise price was so far above the current market price that the likelihood of the market price ever exceeding the exercise price was almost nil. For example, suppose NewEconChip awarded its managers stock options with an exercise price of $75 a share when the market price was $75 a share. As the market price rose to, say, $100 a share, these managers were holding valuable options permitting them to buy stock at $75 that was selling for $100. But, suppose the stock price of NewEconChip, like the stock prices of many technology companies in 2000 and 2001, fell, going to $30. Now the options had no value. And if the prospects were such that the company was not likely to again see a stock price of $75 before the options expired, how much use were they for aligning the interests of managers with shareholders?

What many companies did was to effectively reprice the options; in effect, the exercise price was lowered from $75 to $30 a share. (But this was disguised through a variety of legal devices so that it did not violate Internal Revenue Service regulations.) The rationale was that this was necessary in order to motivate the managers. But the critics asked the following question: If repricing is appropriate when stock prices fall, why not when stock prices rise as well?

CHAPTER 9

THE CORPORATE
CONTROL MARKET

INTRODUCTION

The corporate control market is a market in which investor/management teams buy and sell corporations and compete for control of a company. Narrowly defined, the corporate control market is a corporate takeover market in which mergers, acquisitions, hostile takeovers, leveraged buyouts (LBOs), and management buyouts (MBOs) take place. A broader definition includes a variety of other organizational restructuring events that are related to attempts by one

149

team or another to retain or get control of a company. These events include divestitures, spin-offs, and initial public offerings (IPOs).

WHY A CORPORATE CONTROL MARKET?

Consider LeisurePark Enterprises. LeisurePark has two lines of business: It manufactures canoes, and it owns and operates a chain of motels. Over the years, the canoe business has been quite profitable and has generated considerable cash inflows. In contrast, the motel chain has consistently lost money and has needed cash injections from the canoe business in order to stay afloat. However, even though the motels themselves are money losers, the land on which they are located is quite valuable. In fact, a number of national food franchises have offered to buy the properties from Leisure-Park. But LeisurePark managers have consistently declined to sell the motels.

Now, imagine how investors—especially small public investors—who own stock in LeisurePark feel about this situation. Not only are these investors not receiving the cash dividends that could be paid out of the canoe operations, but, even worse, management is reinvesting the cash in the money-losing motel chain. The result is a lousy stock price. Why not sell the motels, distribute the cash to the public shareholders, and institute cash dividend payments now that the cash flow from the canoe operations is no longer needed to cover the motel losses? It seems pretty simple, right? Well, not if LeisurePark management refuses to sell the motels because it thinks that the motel chain will become profitable in the future or because it believes that it can start its own fast food chain from scratch on the motel properties. So, what alternatives are left for the public shareholders?

They can sell their shares for whatever they can get. But

think about how willing public shareholders would be to buy common stock in any company to begin with if this were the only alternative available to them. With no protection against entrenched managers doing what they wish with the shareholders' money and possibly running down the company merely to buy control of it "on the cheap" themselves, why would public investors buy common stock? Furthermore, this would hardly be a good outcome from a social welfare perspective that seeks to encourage investment in order to generate economic opportunities and growth.

Another alternative would be to try to elect a new and more responsive board of directors. Together with large block holders, the public shareholders could start a proxy fight with an alternative board of directors slate. But for this to happen, both legal provisions that make it possible for the competing management team to gain access to the list of LeisurePark shareholders to ask for their votes and provisions to ensure that the shareholders are able to actually vote their stock must be in place.

A more likely and promising method for removing LeisurePark's entrenched management team is to have a new owner/management team try to gain control of the company by offering to buy the shares of the public investors. Such an offer is called a tender offer, and it involves making a public offer to buy the shares of LeisurePark through advertisements in newspapers and other public media.

A Restructuring Plan for LeisurePark

Figure 9-1 contains relevant financial data for LeisurePark. The assets under the control of the Canoe and Motel Divisions are shown separately, as are the relevant income and cash flow data. The market value of LeisurePark is $225 million, compared to a book value (value of shareholders' equity) of $500 million. On a per share basis, the market price

Figure 9-1   LeisurePark Financial Data (All amounts except per share amounts are in millions of dollars)

	Canoe Division	Motel Division	Total Assets
Cash	$10	$10	$20
Other current assets	70	90	160
Fixed assets	120	300	420
Total assets	**$200**	**$400**	**$600**
Current liabilities	$50	$50	$100
Shareholders' equity (10,000,000 shares outstanding)			$500
Total liabilities and shareholders' equity			$600
Earnings before interest, depreciation, and taxes (EBIDTA)	$92	$10	$102
Depreciation	− $12	− $30	− $42
Earnings before interest and taxes (EBIT)	$80	− $20	$60
Taxes at 40%	− $32	$8	− $24
Net income after taxes	**$48**	**− $12**	**$36**
Cash flow after taxes	$60	$18	$78
Cash flow before taxes	$92	$10	$102
Total market value of equity			$225
Market-to-book ratio			0.45
Per share stock price			$22.50
Earnings per share	$4.80	− $1.20	$3.60
P/E ratio			6.25

is $22.50 a share and the book value is $50.00, for a market-to-book ratio of 0.45.

At least on the basis of book values, investors would be better off if the company were liquidated and the cash distributed to the shareholders. Better yet, the company could just sell off the Motel Division. If the assets of the Motel Division were sold for their book value, the public investors would find themselves in the following position:

- ❒ Cash would increase by $400 million, or $40 a share.
- ❒ The company would no longer operate motels, so no losses would be experienced and net income for the restructured company would be $48 million, or $4.80 per share.
- ❒ If the same P/E ratio of 6.25 remains after selling off the Motel Division, the per share stock price would be $30.
- ❒ The overall effect of restructuring LeisurePark would be to increase the wealth of the existing shareholders by $50 a share. The shareholders would have stock worth $30 a share plus a cash payment from the sale of the Motel Division of $40 a share, and these together would be $47.50 more than the current stock price of $22.50 per share.

A Tender Offer for LeisurePark

How can this be brought about? Well, as long as a market for corporate control exists, competing owner/manager teams can offer to buy the outstanding shares of LeisurePark for up to $70 a share and still come out ahead (ignoring transaction costs and bridge financing charges). At $70 a share, they would break even. Here's a skeleton description of how the process would work.

The new team, call it TicoCap, would accumulate up to 5

percent of LeisurePark shares (500,000 shares) at the current
$22.50 market price, for an investment of $11.25 million.
Then, under U.S. securities law, it would have to announce
that it had accumulated a 5 percent stake in the company. At
this point, TicoCap would offer to buy LeisurePark shares
for, say, $50 a share (or any amount up to $70 a share).
Public investors would then have the choice of tendering
their shares to TicoCap for $50 or keeping them, realizing
that their market value would be $22.50 as long as the en-
trenched management team remained in place. If the public
shareholders tender their shares at $50, TicoCap gains con-
trol of LeisurePark and implements the restructuring plan.
TicoCap makes a capital gain of $23.75 million on the
500,000 shares it bought prior to its tender offer plus the
difference between $70 and whatever price it paid for the
tendered shares.

If the existing management of LeisurePark opposes the
takeover with the backing of the board, the event is called a
hostile takeover (hostile to the entrenched management, not
hostile to the public shareholders). In the next chapter we
describe the strategies that management can use to counter a
hostile takeover. However, one strategy available to Leisure-
Park management is simply to implement the financial program advocated by TicoCap. TicoCap won't be too unhappy
about this because it will still walk away with the $23.75 mil-
lion capital gain on its 5 percent position, even though it
won't get control of the company and the benefits that go
with it. The public shareholders will also be happy because
they will see the stock price rise to $70 a share.

But suppose LeisurePark's management still doesn't
budge. Is it fair to the public investors for TicoCap to pay
them less than $70 a share for their stock? Well, we'll finesse
that question this way: Once TicoCap makes its offer, other
competing management teams are likely to enter the bidding
if TicoCap's tender offer price is too low. In other words,

competition in the corporate control market will drive the price for control of LeisurePark toward $70 a share. For a realistic example, consider the bid General Electric made for Honeywell in October 2000. Prior to the GE bid, United Technologies had offered to pay $50 a share for Honeywell. A few days later, GE came in with a bid worth $54.99 a share and won the auction. Eventually, the European Union antitrust regulators prohibited the merger, so Honeywell remains an independent company. (Apparently United Technologies was no longer interested in the company.) In March 2002, Honeywell was trading at $40 a share—below the price offered by United Technologies more than a year earlier.

We labeled this section "Why a Corporate Control Market?" The answer is that this market motivates managers to run companies in the best interests of the public shareholders; if they do not, someone else may try to gain control of the company. From a broader perspective, the corporate control market serves to ensure that companies use resources effectively and discourages managers from benefiting themselves at the expense of economic growth.

Not everyone agrees that hostile takeovers and a corporate control market are good things or in the best interests of the public. We return to these critiques in our last chapter, which considers comparative corporate governance systems.

MERGERS AND ACQUISITIONS

Mergers and acquisitions result in changes in corporate control. The acquiring company's shareholders either gain control of the target company or, depending on how the deal is structured, share control of the acquiring company with the target company's shareholders. In the case of a merger, an entirely new company may be formed. These corporate control events usually result in major managerial changes as well as changes in and the elimination of corporate boards.

From a public shareholder's perspective, mergers and acquisitions can be and have been value-destroying as well as value-creating. Two common ways of measuring whether a corporate control event created or destroyed value are to look at changes in the market values of the companies on the day of the merger or acquisition announcement and to look at the postmerger performance of the surviving firm.

United Airlines and US Airways

On May 24, 2000, United Airlines (UAL) announced a cash acquisition of US Airways. Figure 9-2 shows what happened to the stock prices and the total market values of the companies around the announcement day. It also includes information on what would be the total market value of the two companies combined, based on their respective stock prices.

We are going to consider this merger from the perspectives of both undiversified and diversified investors. Undiversified investors are those whose shareholdings are concentrated in a few companies or industries. An extreme case would be an

FIGURE 9-2   DATA FOR MERGER OF UAL (UNITED AIRLINES) AND US AIRWAYS, MAY 24, 2000 ANNOUNCEMENT DATE

Date	UAL Stock Price	US Airways Stock Price	Market Value of UAL (billions)	Market Value of US Airways (billions)	Combined Market Value (billions)
May 22, 2000	$59.75	$25.25	$3.178	$1.695	$4.873
May 23, 2000	60.375	26.3125	3.206	1.766	4.972
May 24, 2000	53.1875	49.00	2.824	3.288	6.112
May 25, 2000	52.50	44.625	2.788	2.994	5.782

Shares outstanding: UAL − 53.1 million; US Airways − 67.1 million.

investor who chose to own only UAL stock or only US Airways stock. A fully diversified (also called well-diversified) investor would hold shares in many companies and many different industries. The best example of a fully diversified investor would be someone who owns an index fund such as the Vanguard 500 index fund, a fund that invests in the companies that make up the Standard & Poor's 500 index. Technically, a fully diversified investor owns the market portfolio; in other words, the fully diversified investor owns stock in every publicly traded company and has completely eliminated the unique risks associated with the stocks of the individual companies. The fully diversified investor is left with only the broad economic risks, such as recessions, inflation, and so forth, that affect the performance of all companies. Most reputable investment advisers tell their clients to hold diversified portfolios because the overwhelming evidence is that no one can beat the market. In fact, index mutual funds, which are fully diversified funds, consistently outperform actively managed funds, leaving the index fund investors better off in the long run.

From the perspective of an undiversified US Airways shareholder, the proposed merger was good news. The share price of US Airways rose from $26.3125 prior to the announcement to $49.00 on May 24, generating a percentage gain of 86.2 percent. From the perspective of an undiversified UAL shareholder, the news was terrible. The share price of UAL dropped from $60.375 to $53.1875, for a percentage loss of 11.9 percent.

But what happened from the perspective of a well-diversified investor who owned a proportional amount of both companies—our index fund investor? For this investor, the merger announcement created value. The combined market value of UAL and US Airways rose from $4.972 billion to $6.112 billion, for a gain of 22.93 percent. In other words, investors were saying that these two companies would be worth more together than as separate companies

From the point of view of the economy as a whole, the preferred perspective is that of the fully diversified investor. Overall, the proposed merger seemed to create value. But, note that all the incremental value and then some was received by US Airways shareholders. Eventually this merger also fell victim to regulatory disapproval on antitrust grounds, and US Airways remained an independent company.

Hewlett-Packard and Compaq

A hotly contested and contentious merger that took place in March 2002 was that between Hewlett-Packard and Compaq, announced on September 3, 2001. Hewlett-Packard Company (HP) and Compaq Computer Corporation announced a definitive merger agreement to create what they called an $87 billion global technology leader. Hewlett-Packard management expected the merger to generate cost synergies reaching approximately $2.5 billion annually. Under the terms of the agreement, unanimously approved by both boards of directors, Compaq shareowners were to receive 0.6325 of a newly issued HP share for each share of Compaq, with the companies putting a value of approximately $25 billion on Compaq. So, what did the market think about this?

Not much. Look at Figure 9-3. Prior to the announcement, HP stock traded at $22.93 a share, for a total market value of $44.4842 billion. Compaq stock traded at $12.25, for a market value of $20.825 billion. The combined market value of both companies was $65.3092 billion. After the announcement, the stock price of HP fell by over 18 percent, to $18.77, as did the market value of HP. The stock price of Compaq fell by over 10 percent, as did its market value. The total market value of the two companies was off by over 15 percent, to $55.0968 billion, for a loss of over $10.2 billion.

FIGURE 9-3   HEWLETT-PACKARD (HP) COMPAQ MERGER
ANNOUNCEMENT VALUATION EFFECTS, ANNOUNCEMENT
DATE: SEPTEMBER 3, 2001 (HOLIDAY)

Date	Compaq Stock Price	HP Stock Price	Market Value of Compaq (billions)	Market Value of HP (billions)	Combined Market Value (billions)
Aug 29, 2001	$13.03	$23.66	$22.151	$45.9004	$68.0514
Aug 30, 2001	12.59	23.11	21.403	44.8334	66.2364
Aug 31, 2001	12.25	22.93	20.825	44.4842	65.3092
Sept 4, 2001	10.99	18.77	18.683	36.4138	55.0968
Sept 5, 2001	10.33	17.99	17.561	34.9006	52.4616
Sept 6, 2001	10.27	17.48	17.459	33.9112	51.3702
Sept 7, 2001	10.51	17.86	17.867	34.6484	52.5154
March 14, 2001	$10.70	$19.40	$18.19	$37.636	$55.826

Shares outstanding: Hewlett-Packard 1,700,000,000; Compaq 1,940,000,000.

What happened to those $2.5 billion in after-tax synergies
predicted by management? If we were to conservatively capitalize those annual synergies at 20 percent, the total market
value of the combined companies should have increased by
$12.5 billion; instead, it fell by $10.2 billion—a managerial
forecasting error of $22.7 billion! Yet the management of
both companies continued to press ahead with the merger,
despite the market's assessment and that of a number of institutional investors, including Calpers.

When Do Mergers Create Value?

Was the market's reaction to the UAL–US Airways and HP–
Compaq mergers typical? In some ways, yes; in others, no.
What is clear is that the stock price of the target company
usually increases because the acquiring company is willing to
pay a premium over the target's current price (an "above

market" price). On average, this premium is 20 percent of the target company's preacquisition stock price. The stock price of the acquiring company can go up or down; the average across many merger and acquisition events during the 1980s and 1990s was zero (no change). As to whether the market value of the combined companies went up, the answer is generally yes, although there were numerous exceptions; the AOL–Time Warner deal in 2000, the AT&T–NCR deal in 1991 (which was subsequently undone), and the Digital Equipment–Compaq deal are classic examples. So, what can we make of these empirical findings by financial economists?

When the combined market value of both companies increases, the interpretation is that investors believe that the acquisition or merger makes economic sense because it will produce synergies. Such synergies could arise from economies of scale and scope, reductions in operating costs, and reductions in risk beyond those available to the public investor through portfolio diversification.

Mergers and acquisitions are also often touted as ways for reducing excess capacity in a mature or declining industry. For example, after the end of the Cold War, many mergers and acquisitions took place in the defense industry as military and weapons systems spending wound down. Northrop Corporation acquired Grumman, Lockheed acquired Martin Marietta, and Boeing acquired McDonnell-Douglas.

Who captures the value of merger and takeover synergies? The evidence suggests that it is the target company's shareholders (and, by implication, investors holding well-diversified portfolios, provided that the combined value of the two companies goes up). The price of the target company almost always increases—and by a substantial amount. And this raises an interesting question: Why is the acquirer willing to buy the company at a price that leaves the market value of the acquiring company unchanged? We suspect the answer is that in a competitive corporate control market, the buyer has to give virtually all of the synergistic benefits to the target company; if it does not, another buyer will join the bidding and offer a higher price. And this raises an even more interesting question: Why is the acquiring company willing to pay more than anyone else for the target company?

For the target company to be worth more to the acquirer than to anyone else, the acquirer must believe that there are unique synergies between itself and the target. By unique, we mean synergies that are not available to anyone else. If the forecasted synergies fail to materialize, the shareholders of the acquiring company will bear all of the costs of overpaying the target company shareholders. However, if the target company was acquired with the stock of the acquiring company, the shareholders of both the acquiring company and the old target company will share the losses. This sharing of losses explains why the stock price of both Compaq and Hewlett-Packard fell when the proposed consolidation was announced.

How Can Mergers Destroy Shareholder Value?

Lastly, let's turn to the question of why the acquiring company's stock price might fall. One reason is simply that the acquiring company has offered to pay too high a price for the target. But there are other reasons more akin to corporate governance issues involving conflicts of interest between shareholders and managers.

The managers of firms in mature or declining industries often face limited or even negative growth opportunities. So, how can these managers retain their jobs? One way is go out and buy another company in some other industry, preferably a growth company. Whether the managers have any skills applicable to running such a company is doubtful, and it is even more doubtful that there are unique synergies between the declining firm and the growth industry. Investors generally are skeptical of such acquisitions and drive down the price of the "old-line" acquiring firm.

Another governance-related reason is the relative ease of allocating capital internally across newly acquired divisions rather than relying on the capital markets. For example, once a previously independent company becomes a division of a much larger bureaucracy, internal politics and logrolling may have more to do with allocating scarce capital within the company than the profitability of projects and divisions. Economists call these costs transaction costs, and they are positively related to the size of a bureaucracy and its ability to avoid the discipline of capital markets.

Finally, transparency issues with respect to the true profitability of individual divisions arise as more and more different activities are brought under the control of a single company. As investors become less and less certain about the cash flows from the various parts of the company, they underprice the firm relative to what the total price would have been had the units been stand-alone independent firms.

The aforementioned governance issues, as luck would have it, lead us to our next class of control events. These events are divestitures, spin-offs, LBOs, and MBOs.

DIVESTITURES, SPIN-OFFS, AND CARVE-OUTS

Think of divestitures and spin-offs as demergers. A divestiture is the direct sale of a division or assets, usually to another company. A spin-off is the separation of a division from the company by turning the division into an independent company and then distributing the shares to the parent company's shareholders. A variation of a spin-off is a carve-out, whereby the parent sells all or a portion of the shares in a division to other investors.

Both spin-offs and carve-outs are usually associated with increases in the parent company's stock price on the announcement dates. Thus, investors generally regard the divisions as being worth more as separate companies than as parts of a larger company or a conglomerate. Companies that announce spin-offs and equity carve-outs can generate an increase in the stock value of the parent company of 3 to 4 percent on average.

For example, on October 8, 1997, Ford Motor Company said that it would distribute (spin off) shares in Associates First Capital Corporation, Ford's consumer and commercial lending operation, to its shareholders. Ford said that it was doing so in order to persuade investors that Ford stock was undervalued because investors had failed to value the company's financial businesses appropriately. Ford management believed that investors were putting too low a P/E ratio on its Associates First Capital operation and that if Associates were spun off, the market value of Ford and Associates as separate companies would be greater than their market value together as a single company. Alex Trotman, Ford's chairman and chief executive, said, "We believe the market value of the Associates is neither fully nor consistently reflected in Ford's stock price. . . . Because the market views Ford as an automotive company, it has not fully recognized or rewarded us for our diversification in nonautomotive financial services businesses." Ford said that its plan would be to distribute roughly one share of Associates stock for every four shares of Ford stock. On October 9, 1997, Ford stock went from $48.25 to $49.50 a share, for a one-day gain of 2.6 percent— the sort of gain typically associated with spin-offs.

Earlier in 1997, Ford, through an IPO, had sold off (in contrast to distributing to its shareholders) nearly a fifth of the Hertz Corporation. And, in 1996, General Motors had cut loose the Electronic Data Systems Corporation, which previously had traded as a special class of GM stock.

Why spin-offs and carve-outs? Well, as Ford management said, investors may be undervaluing parts of the company. Investors may simply not have sufficient information about the cash flows coming from various divisions of the company to evaluate the true worth of each division. Or, investors may fully understand where the cash is coming from within the company but be concerned about where the cash is going. In the case of Ford, investors may have feared that the cash from Associates was being used to subsidize automotive operations rather than being distributed as cash dividends.

Sometimes divestitures are done by selling stock in the divested division to the public rather than by selling the division to another company or spinning it off to shareholders. In June 2001, Kraft was spun off from Philip Morris through an initial public offering of 28,000,000 shares. Philip Morris, however, retains approximately 84 percent ownership of the company.

GOING PUBLIC: IPOS

The decision to sell stock to the public for the first time is called going public; the new issue is called an IPO, for initial public offering. Going public is a major corporate governance event; it brings in public shareholders and, as a result, increases any conflicts of interest between managers and owners or among owners that already exist.

Why Go Public?

There are many reasons for going public. Among them are the company's need for additional capital, a desire for investment diversification on the part of the existing owners, and a way for venture capitalists and others who have financed start-ups to exit (recover their original investment and receive their capital gains). But, for virtually all the reasons that are typically offered, a sticky question remains: Why go public instead of selling to a trade buyer (another company)? Some typical answers are that the founders want to retain control of the company but need cash to grow the firm and that the company is worth more as an independent company than as part of a larger firm. The second argument is the same one that we encountered with spin-offs and carve-outs: The firm will perform better as an independent company focusing on its core business than as part of a large corporate bureaucracy.

Another way to understand why firms go public is to adopt a political economy or social policy perspective. From an American perspective, going public is an arrangement that lets individuals obtain the full value of their entrepreneurial efforts. It is simply an extension of the important role of markets in permitting Americans to escape the dependency associated with economic oligarchies and/or governments. From this perspective, the option of going public is more important than the act itself and needs to be understood in a historical-political context in which the option to go public contributes to the formation of new firms by ensuring that entrepreneurs receive full value for their efforts at developing new products and technologies.

LBOS AND MBOS

Going private is the opposite of going public: The public shareholders are bought out, leaving the company in the hands of the buyout group. The term *LBO (leveraged buyout)* is often used in connection with going private because the buyout group usually borrows a substantial sum of money to buy out the public shareholders, thereby putting the company in a highly leveraged position. MBO stands for management buyout. Often the buyout group in a LBO is the existing management, especially if only a division of the company is acquired and taken private.

Why LBOs and MBOs?

LBOs and MBOs dramatically alter the governance structure of a company. For MBOs, conflicts of interests—agency costs—between managers and public shareholders disappear because the managers are now owners and public shareholders no longer exist. For LBOs in general, management (either the old or the new) usually ends up with a sizable equity interest in the company and nonmanagement ownership is very concentrated. The governance benefits of LBOs and MBOs arise from the reduction of agency costs between shareholders and managers, aligning the interests of managers with those of the new owners through high-powered pay schemes and forcing the new manager/owners to run the company as efficiently as possible in order to service the principal and interest payments on the debt used to buy out the public.

Of course, additional agency costs arise out of conflicts of interests between the owners and the creditors—those who lent the money for the LBO. However, if the financing is structured in such a way that strips of equity and debt are sold to the same investor, these conflicts are mitigated because now the owners and the creditors are the same people. This is called unification of security ownership, and it follows from the insights of financial economists about why financial structure does and does not matter.

But what about efficiency gains? Generally, the ratio of cash flow to sales increases, as do sales per employee. The ratio of investment to sales usually decreases and so does the number of employees. As for the creditors—well, sometimes they lose and sometimes they don't, with the difference being determined by whether the takeover premium paid to the public shareholders was on the high side or the low side of the 20 percent mean premium.

Potential Problems for Public Investors

Public shareholders, at least in countries with strong investor protection laws, have gained from LBOs. The stock price of companies that announce that they are going private typically increases by 20 percent or more on the announcement day. Whether the buyout team should have paid the public more, though, is always debatable. Two MBO deals in 2000 provide examples of situations in which some public investors believed that the management buyout team did not get the best price for the shareholders.[1]

Agribrands International decided to sell a division, Ralcorp Holdings, to its managers for $420 million. However, the management of Agribrands did not seek bidders for the division other than Ralcorp management. The potential conflict raised by some public investors is that the same person is chairman of Agribrands and of Ralcorp, and so, in a sense, the buyer and the seller are the same person. Some public investors believed that the board of Agribrands should have looked at other potential buyers for Ralcorp.

Another example cited in the press is the LBO of IBP, Incorporated. IBP management also chose to forgo looking for other buyers for the company. This decision troubled some public shareholders because the IBP buyout group included some of its current managers and board members as well as public investors, who will become private investors after the LBO. None of these investors, including the public investors who will retain their position in the company, has a motivation to pay the public investors who sell their shares to the buyout group as high a price as possible.

Only in transparent and competitive corporate control markets can public investors be reasonably sure that they are not being taken because competing bids are also possible, as happened in the classic RJR–Nabisco merger. The IBP and Agribrands buyouts have raised questions in the financial press about the transparency and competitiveness of the deals.

CHAPTER 10

THE BOARD OF DIRECTORS AND SHAREHOLDER RIGHTS

INTRODUCTION

Corporations in the United States are incorporated under state law. Under these laws, the board of directors is responsible for managing the affairs of the company in the best interests of the shareholders—as interpreted by the courts of that state, of course. So, how should the board be selected, organized, and monitored by shareholders to ensure that their interests remain supreme? And to what extent can boards enhance or dilute the rights of shareholders through such strategies as changing the governance structures and the bylaws of the company?

A HISTORICAL PERSPECTIVE

Public shareholders, especially dispersed shareholders, need some institution or mechanism to monitor and evaluate managerial performance and to protect their ownership interests in the company. The board of directors has evolved to fulfill this function. The directors are elected by the shareholders and, under state law, are expected to demonstrate unyielding loyalty to the company's shareholders (the duty of loyalty) and exercise due diligence in making decisions (the duty of care). However, the extent to which directors have effectively done so is hotly disputed and open to interpretation, especially since the Enron bankruptcy.

There is a fairly widespread consensus that for most of the twentieth century, board membership was more like membership in an exclusive private club, with the board members being effectively appointed by and beholden to management. However, in the late 1980s and 1990s, changes took place in the roles and activism of boards. These changes can be traced to a constellation of events.

From World War II to the 1970s

From the end of World War II until the early 1970s, the U.S. economy performed fairly well. U.S. multinationals dominated many markets, and, at least in the 1960s, many Europeans were fearful of American domination of their markets and cultures. These years marked the peak of managerial capitalism. But then came the Vietnam War, the OPEC oil embargo, and the stagflation of the 1970s. The U.S. economy was performing poorly in relative terms, especially compared to Japan. The stock of large U.S. corporations was selling for less than book value, suggesting that these companies were worth more dead than alive. Stock prices languished throughout the 1970s and into the 1980s, causing investors, especially institutional investors, to become increasingly disenchanted with corporate America's performance.

Boards Again Attract Attention

Some people, of whom perhaps the chief spokesperson was Michael Porter, attributed the anemic performance of the U.S. economy to a faulty corporate governance system that forced managers to focus on share prices rather than on the long-term interests of the company.[1] Others thought that the cure advocated by Porter was the disease: Managers and boards had become too cozy and weren't paying enough attention to stock prices.[2] The solutions advocated and implemented by these people were hostile takeovers, LBOs, proxy fights, and recommendations to boards of poorly performing companies concerning corporate governance reforms and ways to improve the boards' operation. Institutional investors led the way with respect to governance reforms and "best practices" for boards of directors.

The critiques of both camps—Porter and the advocates of a strong corporate control market—led to many of the changes that were observed in the 1990s. In particular, independent directors (those who are not managers of the company) now make up a majority of the board at large publicly traded firms, and board committees have been created or restructured to better serve the public shareholders.

Among the most influential actors with regard to changes

in the board of directors and other governance reforms have been TIAA-CREF and Calpers. TIAA-CREF is the Teachers Insurance and Annuity Association—College Retirement Equity Fund; it manages billions of dollars in pension fund contributions. Calpers is the California Public Employees Retirement System; it manages pension money for the state of California. Calpers is the largest public pension fund in the nation and the third largest in the world, with assets totaling more than $166 billion. It is very active in corporate governance issues, both in the United States and elsewhere.

TIAA-CREF, Calpers, and many other institutional investors and public interest groups generally agree on what constitutes an effective board of directors and the policies these directors should follow. As shown in Figure 10-1, these institutional investors have become increasingly important in the United States. From 1990 through 2000, they have increased their ownership of U.S. equities from 31.3 percent to 41.7 percent of outstanding shares. We now turn to the policies they recommend.[3]

COMPOSITION AND COMPENSATION OF THE BOARD OF DIRECTORS

A company's board of directors should have a substantial majority of independent directors. These should be individuals with no connection to the company other than a seat on the board, thus minimizing any conflicts of interest with respect to having responsibility for managing the company and simultaneously evaluating and selecting management. The directors' loyalty should be entirely to the shareholders.

In principle, the requirement that independent directors "have no connection" should exclude not only all full-time employees, but also family and friends of employees and the

FIGURE 10-1   OWNERSHIP OF U.S. EQUITIES: 1990 AND 2000

Ownership group	1990		2000	
	Billions of $	Percentage	Billions of $	Percentage
Household sector	$1,796.0	50.7%	$6,575.7	38.3%
Bank personal trusts and estates	191.0	5.4%	309.0	1.8%
Life insurance companies	81.5	2.3%	944.3	5.5%
Other insurance companies	81.5	2.3%	171.7	1.0%
Institutional investors	1,109.0	31.3%	7,159.5	41.7%
Private pension funds	605.9	17.1%	1,991.6	11.6%
State and local retirement funds	269.3	7.6%	1,940.1	11.3%
Mutual funds	233.8	6.6%	3,227.8	18.8%
Rest of the world	244.4	6.9%	1,716.9	10.0%
Other	39.6	1.1%	291.0	1.7%
Total	$3,543.0	100.0%	$17,168.1	100.0%

Source: U.S. Census Bureau, *Statistical Abstract of the United States* (Washington, D.C.: U.S. Government Printing Office, 2001).

company's lawyers, accountants, bankers, suppliers, and customers. However, since these people often have positive contributions to make to the success of the company, they will often be found on boards. Therefore, a third category of director, such as affiliated, is often used; however, these persons do not qualify as outside or independent directors in determining whether the board has a substantial majority of outside members.

Board Committees

The board should have audit, compensation, and nominating committees made up entirely of outside directors. Furthermore, those committees that are assigned the task of board evaluation, governance, compliance, and ethics should also have only outside members.

The audit committee ensures that the books aren't being cooked and that shareholders are properly informed of the financial status of the firm. Typically, the audit committee recommends the CPA firm that will audit the company's books, reviews the activities of the company's independent accountants and internal auditors, and reviews the company's internal control systems and its accounting and financial reporting requirements and practices.

The compensation committee normally does the following: (1) recommends the selection of the CEO, (2) reviews and approves the appointment of officers who report directly to the CEO, (3) reviews and approves the compensation of the CEO and the managers reporting to the CEO, and (4) administers the stock compensation and other incentive plans.

The nominating committee establishes qualifications for potential directors. It also puts together a list of candidates for board membership for the shareholders to vote on. In all these cases, the point of having only outside directors is to prevent management from concealing information, deciding on its own pay, and gaining effective control of the company by controlling the board election process.

Diversity should be an important factor in constructing a board. The members should all be qualified individuals, but there should be a diversity of experience, gender, race, and age. However, diversity should not be construed to mean that directors should represent special interests. Instead, the directors should represent all the shareholders. We return to this issue in the section on electing board members, where we explain cumulative voting.

Board Compensation

Compensation for members of the board of directors continues to be a controversial topic. Two issues are bound together. One is how the board members should be compensated. The other is how much time they should spend in their role as directors, which is related to how and how much they should be paid.

A member of a large corporation's board of directors will normally be paid between $20,000 and $30,000 a year plus fees to cover expenses for traveling to meetings. For example, in 1999 outside directors of C.R. Bard received an annual retainer of $26,000 cash plus $1,200 for each board and committee meeting attended (the committee chair gets $2,400). An additional $4,400 is either paid in common stock based on the stock's fair market value or added to deferred compensation plans. In 1999, nonemployee directors of Heinz received $30,000 in cash and 300 shares of common stock. In addition, they received $3,000 for each board or committee meeting attended.

Now for the interesting pay question. Why should the outside board members devote time and effort to representing the public shareholders if they have no stake in the company? We have often said that a way to align management's interests with those of the shareholders is to tie executive pay to the stock price or to have managers own shares in the company. So, why shouldn't the same arrangement(s) be instituted for outside board members? Why not require independent directors to own stock in the company and tie their pay to performance as well?

To some extent, this concern explains the pay schemes we noted for C.R. Bard and Heinz, where board members receive stock as well as cash, and that for United Industrial Corporation in 2000, where each director was granted an option to purchase 15,000 shares of common stock upon the director's initial appointment to the board. In fact, between 1995 and 2000, directors' compensation in the form of stock rose from 28 percent to over 60 percent for the "average" company.[4]

TIAA-CREF says that "a reasonable minimum ownership interest could be defined as stock holdings equal to approximately one-half of the amount of the director's annual retained fee." But still, we would suggest that for many board members, the amount of stock they own in, say, Heinz or United Industrial Corporation is small relative to their overall wealth and is not sufficient to do much in terms of changing their behavior.

With respect to time spent on the job, a common criticism of U.S. boards is that too often the members hold positions on so many boards that they can't possibly devote the time and attention necessary to carry out their responsibilities to the shareholders. For example, in 1992, an ex–U.S. Secretary of Defense served on the boards of more than twenty for-profit companies and many not-for-profit organizations. The question is how someone, no matter how talented, would have the time to do the job properly for so many companies while still holding a full-time position as well. Therefore, when nominating committees select potential board members, we think they should consider the candidates' other responsibilities relative to time demands. The rule of thumb that seems to be used is that to do the job properly, a board member needs to devote at least 100 hours annually to the job, although in recent years, with the increased public scrutiny of boards, more hours are probably devoted to the job.

What about other forms of board compensation or quasi compensation? Should board members accept consulting fees from the firm? What about having the company make donations to a board member's favorite charity? Clearly, both of these payments raise conflict of interest issues.

Tyco Corporation offers a recent example of a board member receiving consulting fees as well as having the company donate money to a selected charity. Tyco International paid a total of $20 million to an outside director and to a charity he controls, in return for his help in brokering a

major acquisition in 2001. The move drew fire from corporate governance experts, who have advocated more director
independence from top management. According to Tyco's
annual proxy statement, director Frank E. Walsh, Jr. received
a $10 million cash fee because he was "instrumental in bring-
ing about" Tyco's $9.5 billion acquisition of finance com-
pany CIT Group. Tyco also made a $10 million contribution
to a New Jersey charitable fund of which Walsh is trustee.[5]

Similar donations appear to have been made by Enron.[6]
On October 31, 2001, Enron named William Powers, Jr.,
dean of the University of Texas Law School, to its board.
Enron announced this appointment the same day it reported
that the Securities and Exchange Commission had opened a
formal investigation into questionable financial transactions
at Enron, including the use of partnerships to hide losses,
and Powers was named chairman of a special committee to
do an internal investigation and respond to the SEC. "We
had a need to have an independent board member chair this
special committee," company spokeswoman Karen Denne
said at the time. However, the appointment was criticized
because of the law school's close ties with top Enron officials,
including Enron's general counsel, James V. Derrick, Jr. Derrick had served in key fund-raising positions for the law
school, and Enron had made donations to the law school as
well as to the business school. So, how independent is Powers? From the outside looking in, too many questions can be
raised about implicit connections between Enron and the law
school of which Powers is dean.

Powers is not the only University of Texas insider whose
independence has been questioned. John Mendelsohn is
president of the M. D. Anderson Cancer Center at the University of Texas and a member of Enron's audit committee.
However, M. D. Anderson has received almost $600,000 in
donations from Enron and its CEO, Kenneth Lay, raising

questions about how carefully Mendelsohn was scrutinizing Enron's books for the shareholders.

Another member of Enron's audit committee is Wendy Gramm. Gramm is the director of the Mercatus Center at George Mason University, which has received $50,000 in Enron contributions over five years.

THE CEO AND THE BOARD CHAIR

The board chair is elected by the board members, who, collectively, must select and evaluate the performance of the CEO. If the CEO and the board chair are the same person, an inherent conflict of interest exists. The CEO is effectively selecting and evaluating him- or herself. Nevertheless, at about 75 percent of U.S. companies, the CEO is also the board chair—a situation that is far less common in other countries.

The case for having the CEO and the chair be the same person is one of practicality: Both the CEO and the chair need to be very involved with the business of the company; therefore, combining their roles seems efficient.

SHAREHOLDER RIGHTS

Shareholder rights encompass a wide variety of issues, ranging from voting procedures to rules governing the issuance of new shares, including shares issued for mergers and acquisitions, to access to information, and to the way managers can and do respond to corporate control challenges. We begin with a consideration of voting rights, including a consideration of multiple classes of stock.

Voting Rights

In theory, shareholders control—govern—the corporation through their voting rights. These rights enable the shareholders to elect the board of directors and to vote on those issues that affect shareholder control of the company. In reality, there are many obstacles that make it very difficult for the public shareholders to effectively exercise their franchise.

How Many Votes for Each Shareholder?

Let's begin with the question of how many votes each shareholder should be permitted to cast. As we noted earlier, during the nineteenth century it was not uncommon for shareholders to receive only one vote regardless of the number of shares they owned. This system provided both a way to protect minority interests (those who did not control over 50 percent of the shares) and a way to ensure that the corporation remained socially responsive to local interests, even though the majority of the shares were typically owned by people quite distant from where the company was operating. However, the system had its disadvantages.

The wealth of the major financial contributors to the firm could be held hostage by those with hardly any exposed financial position. How concerned would the small shareholders be with the financial health of the company and its major investors, as opposed to the benefits the company was providing to the local community or to themselves through their nonshareholder connections with the company? In other words, the relationship between the costs of certain investment and financing strategies to the small shareholders and these shareholders' exposed ownership was way out of proportion to the same relationship for those who had committed large amounts of their personal wealth to the firm. So, voting rights began evolving toward the one-share-one-vote system that is most common in the United States today.

Institutional investors involved in corporate governance generally advocate the one-share-one-vote rule. This rule is also often described as the most democratic governance structure. Indeed, the objection to multiple classes of common stock is very similar to the objection to the one-vote-per-owner regime. Multiple classes of shares can be used to separate cash flow rights from control rights. Typically, one group of individuals (usually the founders) retains the control rights and the perks that go with them by holding one class of stock with majority voting rights. They then create a new class of stock with less than 50 percent of the voting rights to sell to the public. The public gets the right to cash flows, but not control of the board and the company. Therefore, the owners of the controlling class can continue to run the company in their own interests, and not those of the public shareholders, without worrying about losing control.

Confidentiality Issues

Advocates of "good" governance also believe that voting should be confidential in order to remove any appearance (or reality) of conflicts of interest, improprieties, or potential retribution involving the existing management and the voters. Consider the following situation: The management of White Pine Products finds itself in the middle of a proxy battle with a group of dissident shareholders for control of the company. A new board has been proposed by the dissident group, and White Pine executives are counting the votes as they come into the company. White Pine executives keep a running tally and know who has voted for and against them. The election is close, and a large block holder, Epsom Benefit Fund, has voted against management. White Pine executives know some of the senior managers of Epsom and call them up to ask them to change their vote. The Epsom managers agree (who knows why, but you can guess), and the votes are changed. Confidential voting would prevent this from happening—or at least reduce the temptation and the likelihood.

ERISA and Institutional Investor Voting Responsibilities

With the passage of the Employee Retirement Income Security Act (ERISA) in 1974 and subsequent legislation and court interpretations of these laws, institutional investors who manage pension funds have increasingly been held accountable for voting their shares in the best interests of the funds' beneficiaries. These laws impose rigorous fiduciary duties on fund managers of employee pension plans.

The Department of Labor has stated that these duties extend to actively monitoring situations in which "the activities of the plan alone, or together with other shareholders, are likely to enhance the value of the plan's investment, after taking into account the costs involved." Furthermore, courts have held that managers of employee stock ownership plans have a duty to pursue the claims of minority shareholders, and have imposed liability on plan fiduciaries for failing to do so. In addition, the Investment Advisers Act of 1940, covering mutual funds, has been interpreted to impose a duty on investment advisers to act as fiduciaries with respect to their customers.

Electing the Board of Directors

Although shareholders elect the board of directors, the process and procedure for doing so matter. We consider two controversial issues: cumulative voting and staggered boards.

Cumulative Voting

Cumulative voting is a way for minority shareholders to elect or increase the likelihood of electing one of their number to the board of directors. Cumulative voting works as follows: Suppose you own 10,000 shares of a company that has 100,000 shares outstanding, or 10 percent of the voting rights, and the corporation has nine people on its board. Without cumulative voting, you would vote for the nine people you wanted, and each person you selected would receive 10,000 votes. In effect, you have 90,000 votes, but you must spread them evenly among the nine candidates.

With cumulative voting, you could take the entire 90,000 votes and award them to a single candidate. Of course, you would not be able to vote for other candidates; however, you could join forces with other like-minded shareholders and elect at least one board member who would represent your views.

People who believe that the directors should represent all shareholders generally oppose cumulative voting. Others see cumulative voting as a way of ensuring that all shareholder views will be represented, not just the views of those who own a controlling interest.

Staggered Boards

Until the market for corporate control heated up in the 1980s, most boards were elected to coterminous annual terms. For example, the 1999 Heinz proxy statement says that seventeen members will be elected to the board and serve for one year.

Staggered boards were developed as a means of fending off hostile takeovers. The process works as follows: People's Heritage Financial Group, Inc., a Portland, Maine–based bank, has fifteen board members. The board is divided into three classes of five directors each. One class of directors is elected each year for a three-year term. Thus, in any given year, only one-third of the board is up for election. Consequently, a competing owner-management team could never elect a majority of the board and thereby gain control of People's Heritage in a single year. At least two years would have to go by. And even if a competing team controlled over 50 percent of the shares of People's Heritage, they would be stuck with a board that was still dominated by the old management.

Today, staggered boards are very common; perhaps as many as half of the publicly traded companies have this arrangement. The argument in favor of staggered boards is that continuity is needed, but why did continuity become necessary only in the 1990s? Another argument, and one that we find more convincing, is that staggered boards may result in higher acquisition premiums being offered to shareholders in order to convert a hostile takeover to a friendly takeover by getting the approval of the existing board.

POISON PILLS, SUPERMAJORITY RULES, AND GREENMAIL

Poison pills and supermajority rules are devices that management can use to defend itself against a hostile takeover, although a case can be made that such devices may also benefit shareholders. Greenmail refers to premium payments made to individuals to get them to stop trying to gain control of the company. Supermajority rules simply require that more than 50 percent of the shareholders approve a merger or sale of the company. Typically, the percentage is two-thirds, but it could be as high as 90 percent. Naturally, the higher the percentage, the easier it is for the existing management team to retain control of the company.

Poison pills are corporate charter provisions, financial security issues, or other contractual provisions that either transfer wealth or ownership from the takeover group to the target company's shareholders or force the takeover group to pay off a substantial debt if the takeover succeeds. For example, if the managers of Downwest Bank wanted to make it difficult for an outside group to gain control of the bank, they could issue rights to buy preferred shares in Downwest to the existing shareholders of Downwest. In the event of a hostile takeover of Downwest, these rights would be convertible into the shares of the acquiring company at a bargain price. These provisions are called shareholder rights plans, although critics have dubbed them management rights plans.

A Shareholder Rights Plan at First Virginia Banks (FVA)

In 2001, FVA had a shareholder rights plan that effectively gave common shareholders a right to buy for $450 common stock in the company having a market value of $900 in the event that a person or entity were to acquire 20 percent or more of FVA's common stock. However, the rights would not be exercisable if the stock were acquired at a price and on terms determined by the board of directors to be adequate and in the best interests of the shareholders. The effect of this poison pill is to make any hostile takeover of FVA very expensive to the competing control team.

Evidence About Antitakeover Devices

What is the evidence regarding the effect of these antitakeover devices? Well, the general consensus is that the majority of these provisions hurt shareholders, although exceptions occur. Generally speaking, institutional investors oppose these provisions. TIAA-CREF's corporate governance policies say that:

❐ The board should submit any antitakeover measure for prior shareholder approval.

❑ The board should oppose any action to adopt superma-jority rules.

❑ The board should require equal financial treatment for all shareholders and limit the company's ability to buy back shares from certain investors at higher-than-market prices (greenmail).

BOARD GOVERNANCE AND FIRM PERFORMANCE

Numerous academic studies have been undertaken in recent years in an effort to determine whether many of the issues we covered in this chapter are, in reality, related to firm performance. The evidence turns out to be mixed, and the jury remains out. But, little by little, evidence is accumulating that suggests that governance reforms and the increasing focus on governance issues have affected corporate investment and financing decisions and have brought shareholder concerns to the forefront.

Indicative of the accumulating evidence is a 1998 study by Paul W. MacAvoy and Ira M. Millstein of the performance of companies that responded to a Calpers corporate governance survey of 300 companies that asked whether the boards had reviewed and adopted governance procedures thought to be consistent with the long-term interests of shareholders. Calpers gave the responses grades from A to F. What MacAvoy and Millstein did was to take these grades and compare them to the company's EVA.[7] They concluded that "over [the 1991–1995 period] the 63 companies receiving the highest Calpers grade achieved average annual, industry-adjusted returns on capital that were 700 basis points higher than the returns on the 44 firms rated 'C.'"

Do we know anything else? Well, no theory of boards—

corporate or otherwise—yet exists, even though boards have been around for hundreds of years and have been subjected for years to the same criticisms of how well they function and who they really represent that are heard today. Back in 1776, Adam Smith had already noted that the directors (boards) of joint stock companies should not be expected to be as vigilant in watching over other people's money as in watching over their own. It turns out that he was quite right!

What we do have are stylized facts. Among these are the fact that despite the attention accorded to outside board membership, there is little evidence that firm performance is positively correlated with the ratio of inside to outside board members. What is positively correlated with the outside-to-inside ratio is the likelihood that the board will adopt governance policies approved by institutional investors with regard to executive pay, poison pills, and mergers and acquisitions. With regard to actual financial performance, though, what does seem to matter is the size of the board: The smaller the board, the better the firm's performance.

We also believe that boards have become more active in replacing CEOs than in the past. Through the first ten months of 2000, thirty-eight of the country's largest corporations replaced their CEOs, compared with only twenty-three during all of 1999 and fewer in the 1980s. The companies doing so included Campbell Soup, Procter & Gamble, Gillette, Lucent Technologies, and Mattel.

CHAPTER 11

ALTERNATIVE GOVERNANCE SYSTEMS: GERMANY AND JAPAN

INTRODUCTION

The American corporate governance system is a market-based system. Corporations raise funds in public capital markets, and their managers are subject to the discipline of capital markets. Theoretically, a company is run in the best interests of its shareholders, whose interests are considered to be "above" those of the other stakeholders of the company. Banks provide debt capital but do not own shares of companies and deal with borrowers at arms length.

The two major alternatives to the American governance system are the German system and the Japanese system (the governance systems of other countries are variations on the American, German, or Japanese system). The German system is a bank-based system, often referred to as a universal banking system. The Japanese system is one of cross-ownership of firms and interlocking relationships called *keiretsu*. Both systems are also described as relationship-oriented systems.

THE GERMAN SYSTEM

The ownership of German corporations is far more concentrated than the ownership of U.S. corporations. Furthermore, as we showed in Figure 2-3, more than 40 percent of the shares in German companies are owned by other German companies. Individuals own very few shares of public corporations, and, for all practical purposes, no institutional investors (mutual funds, pension funds) exist. In short, Germany does not have a shareholder culture. The market capitalization of listed stocks in Germany is about 30 percent of gross national product, compared to 152 percent in the United Kingdom, 122 percent in the United States, and 103 percent in Sweden.

Another major difference between the American system and the German system is the role of banks. In the United States, banks make loans to corporations but do not take ownership positions in those firms (own shares of stock in the company). In Germany, though, banks can and do take ownership positions in the companies they lend to, and also place their representatives on the companies' governing boards. Thus, there is a much closer and stronger relationship between German firms and German banks than there is between American firms and American banks. This relationship is buttressed by the fact that shares owned by Germans are usually deposited in banks for safekeeping and that the banks get to vote these shares, even though they don't own them.

German Governing Boards

Unlike U.S. firms, German corporations have two governing boards: a supervisory board (*Aufsichtsrat*) and a management board (*Vorstand*). The management board is made up of five to fifteen full-time employees of the company and is responsible for the operations of the company. The management board is appointed by the supervisory board and reports to it. All major investment and financing decisions must be approved by the supervisory board.

The supervisory board consists of from nine to twenty-two members. Perhaps most importantly from a governance perspective, the supervisory board is required by law to have labor representatives as well as shareholder representatives. Labor representatives make up one-third of the supervisory boards of corporations with less than 2,000 employees and one-half of the supervisory boards of corporations with more than 2,000 employees. The other board members are elected by the shareholders. But, since over 50 percent of outstanding shares are controlled by other companies and banks with commercial relationships to the company, a conclusion that the boards of German companies represent public shareholders is unwarranted.

This subordination of shareholder interests to the interests of other stakeholders is reinforced by German law with respect to the responsibilities of supervisory board members.

Supervisory board members are not liable for management decisions that are detrimental to shareholder interests, as they would be in the United States under the "duty of care" rules. In other words, whatever the supervisory board is, it is not a creature representing or charged with representing the primacy of shareholder interests.

Absence of Corporate Control Market

Along with the absence of a well-developed capital market, there is an absence of a corporate control market in Germany. Through 1995, there had been only three hostile bids since the end of World War II. Indeed, the whole idea of a corporate control market is near anathema to many Germans. This attitude is aptly captured in the public statements of Gerhard Schroeder, the German chancellor, during the eventually successful hostile takeover of Mannesmann by Vodafone Air Touch in 1999–2000. Schroeder noted that "hostile bids destroyed the culture of the target company . . . [and] hostile bidders in German companies underestimate the virtue of codetermination [worker representation on supervisory boards]." Schroeder, again in response to the Mannesmann takeover, also said that "hostile takeovers are never helpful."

With Germany's Euro-MPs at the forefront of opposition, the European Parliament rejected a cross-border code for takeovers in July 2001. As reported in the *Economist*,

> The failure is a blow for economic liberalisers, who saw it as a key part of their strategy for sharpening economic competition within the European Union. The thrust of the directive was to make it harder for European corporate bosses to ward off a hostile bid without first consulting shareholders. The idea was

that shareholder rights would be strengthened, and managers forced to become more efficient.[1]

German recalcitrance with respect to takeovers continued in 2002. In February 2002, Schroeder warned the European Commission to keep its hands off VW, a carmaker that is the country's largest employer. He is quoted as saying, "Any efforts by the commission in Brussels to smash the VW culture will meet the resistance of the federal government as long as we are in power."[2]

So, do all of these governance differences matter? And why?

UNIVERSAL BANKING: A GERMAN GOVERNANCE SOLUTION

Let's start with what many people believe or believed to be the advantages of the German system compared to the American system. Most of the potential advantages are thought to arise out of a reduction in agency costs and conflicts of interest among the owners and creditors of German firms.

The essence of the German universal banking system is that German banks can own equity in the companies to which they lend money. Consequently, conflicts of interest between creditors and shareholders are reduced because the creditors and the shareholders are the same people. We encountered this idea earlier when we explained the connections between governance and financing decisions.

Advantages of Universal Banking

Conflicts of interests between creditors and shareholders are most likely to surface during periods of financial distress, when the borrower has insufficient cash to make principal and interest payments on debt obligations. Borrowers can play many games during periods of financial distress, such as changing the firm's investment policies (to favor high-risk projects), borrowing additional funds to keep the firm afloat, paying cash dividends rather than paying down debt, not disclosing the financial difficulties to creditors, and restructuring the firm without gaining the approval of the creditors. Creditors are aware of these games and protect themselves by writing positive and negative covenants into loan agreements and by simply refusing to lend more money. Lenders can also force the firm to restructure itself voluntarily, force restructuring through the bankruptcy courts, or ask the courts to liquidate the company.

When banks also own equity in the borrower, the risks associated with the borrower's playing games that transfer wealth from the creditor to the borrower are ameliorated; by owning an equity stake, the bank's losses on its loans are offset by gains on its equity. In addition, lenders who also hold equity positions in a company are less likely than pure creditors to force a firm into bankruptcy when the firm encounters financial problems. Instead, the bank will work with the firm to seek a solution to the problems, since the bank stands to lose its equity position if it calls in the loan but could gain on its equity position if a turnaround can be worked out. The bank, in other words, is a "committed investor."

In theory, these reductions in potential agency, financial distress, and bankruptcy costs should translate into a lower cost of capital for German firms by permitting them to increase their financial leverage and substitute cheap debt financing for expensive debt financing. This potential reduction in cost of capital is reinforced because the banks have representatives on the borrower's board of directors. These bank directors have access to inside information about the company and its financial situation, making it more difficult for the borrower to mislead the bank.

Having bankers on the board and having banks own equity may also reduce the potential costs of financial distress in terms of the company's relationships with customers and suppliers. Customers and suppliers may be more willing to continue doing business with a firm that is in temporary difficulty if they know that a bank is involved and that, because it has an equity stake, it will be reluctant to call in the loan and bankrupt the firm.

Bank membership on borrowers' boards and bank ownership of equity in their borrowers should also, in theory, affect dividend policy and investment policy. We noted that firms with no positive NPV projects should pay cash dividends. But we also noted that in the absence of a corporate control market or other mechanisms to discipline managers, managers might decide to grow the firm at the expense of the shareholders rather than distribute cash to the owners. In the absence of a German corporate control market, banks may be the mechanism that disciplines managers and stops them from making negative NPV investments—but we want to emphasize "may" here because it is not entirely clear whose interests the banks represent. This issue leads us into the disadvantages of the universal banking system.

Disadvantages of Universal Banking

Do German banks protect the interests of the public shareholders, or do German banks primarily protect their own interests in German companies? And, from a broader public policy perspective, what are the implications of the German universal banking system for supporting investments in new technologies and start-ups and for the emergence of public capital markets, especially an IPO market?

Banks May Care About Firm Survival, Not Share Price

Critics of universal banking point out that banks may be more interested in the survival of the firm and its continued existence as a borrower than in maximizing the wealth of public shareholders. Consequently, banks are likely to discourage firms from making risky but positive NPV investments, especially in projects with substantial intangible growth opportunities but no tangible assets. Instead, investment will be directed toward bricks-and-mortar projects, not projects where most of the funds go into human capital and firm-specific assets.

Critics also charge that banks will discourage firms from distributing cash dividends because this cash would leave the company, thus weakening the bank's creditor position. In this regard, banks exacerbate conflicts of interest between the public shareholders and managers because the banks take the side of managers who want to retain control of free cash flow. Banks, in other words, act more like organizational stakeholders such as employees and managers than like public shareholders who discipline managers.

When we recall that over 40 percent of the stock in German firms is owned by other corporations, which themselves are more likely to be interested in the survival of the firm so as to retain the benefits of interfirm commercial contacts, the prospects for protecting the interests of public shareholders in German firms are weak. Banks and other managers control publicly held German firms, with no German institutional investors holding substantial positions on behalf of public investors as in the United States.

Weak Investor Protection Laws

Relatively weak investor protection laws exacerbate the public investors' situation, as does a financial reporting system that is geared more toward taxation issues than toward disclosure. Under German accounting regulations, companies can "smooth" earnings by bypassing the income statement and making transfers to retained earnings in good years and then putting these earnings back into the income statement in bad years.

Some observers have suggested that the reason for the highly concentrated ownership of German firms is weak investor protection. Only large block holders find it possible and worthwhile to monitor and control management, so concentrated ownership has emerged in Germany as an alternative to capital markets for disciplining management and reducing the agency costs associated with the separation of management and ownership.

Absence of an Equity Market Hinders Formation of New Firms

Lastly, the absence of a liquid and efficient equity market may discourage the formation of new firms, especially technology-based firms. Here, the argument turns on the absence of an exit strategy for the founders and venture capitalists. Those who supply capital to start-ups expect to get back their investment plus capital gains. They need what is called an exit strategy. They can exit either by selling the company to a trade buyer (another company) or by taking the company public through an IPO. IPOs require a well-functioning equity market. Without such a market, the only alternative to retaining an interest in the company is selling to another group of private investors or selling to another company. In the former case, the price would be less than with an IPO because this second group of private investors faces as illiquid a market for the company as did the original owners. In the second case, the price might also be less than what public investors would be willing to pay, especially if the buyer knows it is in a commanding market position.

Another problem is that the founders of the company may want to keep the company independent and retain control but don't have enough cash to buy out the venture capitalists. If a well-functioning equity market existed, the founders could take the company public through an IPO and still retain control. But, in the absence of an equity market, the founders may have no alternative but to sell the firm to another company, thus losing the benefits of control.

In both cases, the motivation for starting new companies is diminished. The result is a truncation of investment in new industries and technologies and a brake on entrepreneurial activity.

WHAT'S THE EVIDENCE WITH RESPECT TO GERMANY?

Do the differences between the German and American governance systems generate differences in financial performance? Or, are the systems merely different ways of solving similar problems arising out of the separation of management and ownership, with no substantial differences in terms of overall performance? The evidence is mixed, often qualitative, and frequently controversial.

Although some researchers have found that bank-controlled German companies did not perform as well for their public shareholders as non-bank-controlled companies, others have not been able to show much difference in terms of profitability or share price performance. We do know that IPOs are far less common in Germany than in countries with market-based governance systems, but is the absence of IPOs hindering the economic performance of the overall economy? That is unclear.

Why German Firms Adopt an American Governance Structure

Perhaps the clearest insights into the question of German versus American governance structures can be gained from studying the reasons why a number of large German firms have chosen to move from a German-style governance culture to an American-style governance culture during the last decade. These companies, which coupled the transition with listing themselves on the NYSE, included Daimler-Benz (now DaimlerChrysler), SGL Carbon, Pfeiffer Vacuum, Fresenius Medical Care, Deutsche Telekom, Hoechst (now Aventis after a merger with Rhone-Poulenc), VEBA, and SAP.

Daimler was very explicit about the changes the company made and would make. Daimler adopted the notion of shareholder primacy and implemented stock option plans for its managers. When Juergen Schrempp took over as CEO in 1995, he noted that "those businesses which, after adjusting for risk, fail to earn a pre-tax return of 12% on capital will be dumped." In 1996, Daimler withdrew from Fokker's aircraft business, disposed of its energy systems technology business and its industrial automation business, and sold off other businesses as well.

SGL Carbon is a company that was spun off by Hoechst and listed on the NYSE. On its investor relations Web page in 1999, SGL Carbon stated, "If shareholder value is to be optimally implemented the first requirement is to firmly anchor the philosophy of shareholder value in the minds of management and convert an 'employee-manager' attitude to an 'owner-manager' mentality [through stock options and other incentive plans]." This philosophic statement reflects the shift from a German- to an American-style governance culture.

Pfeiffer Vacuum CEO Wolfgang Dondorf, in commenting

on Pfeiffer's decision to list its stock on the NYSE, stated that using American accounting principles (GAAP) prompted a change in the company's business attitudes by providing more transparency to public investors—another key element of a market-based governance system. Dondorf went on to say that "Pfeiffer believes that its management should turn its attention to increasing the shareholder value of Pfeiffer and should receive remuneration corresponding to the degree to which they achieve this goal."

Deutsche Telekom, the German phone company, was privatized through a listing on the NYSE. Its chief financial officer said at the time that the company was being rationalized "with a view towards competition and shareholder value." Again, the notion of shareholder primacy appears.

Hoechst listed its shares on the NYSE in 1997. Its CEO said, "The Hoechst share price will serve as the yardstick of our performance; in other words, we want the capital markets, specifically you, our shareholders, to be the judge of our efforts."[3]

VEBA switched to GAAP and listed itself on the NYSE in 1997. When it did so, management eliminated limitations on voting rights for shareholders and adopted a one-share-one-vote rule. The chairman also noted that "with our [NYSE listing] we are deliberately exposing ourselves to the critical appraisal of the world's most important capital market and we hope to expand our access to U.S. institutional funds [investors]."[4]

SAP, in adopting U.S. accounting rules, said that it did so because its competitors used GAAP and SAP needed to create a level playing field. It noted that "under German accounting rules, customers have had trouble comparing its financial strength with that of say Oracle—an important consideration in buying very expensive systems meant to last for years."[5]

Whether other German companies will follow these firms

is an open question. But, note that the firms that have moved toward a market-based shareholder-primacy governance structure were competing in global markets and facing competition from American companies. Does this mean that a market-based governance structure is an advantage in such an environment? Or, are the reasons offered by the German companies simply rationalizations for paying managers higher salaries and improving their bargaining position within Germany with respect to workers and social welfare initiatives?

THE JAPANESE *KEIRETSU*

The *keiretsu* is a network of affiliated companies (industrial grouping) formed around a central company or bank and connected through cross-ownership and relational contracting. Examples, past and present, include the Toyota, Mitsubishi, and Mitsui *keiretsu*. The Mitsui Group, originally a producer and seller of soy sauce, is one of Japan's largest *keiretsu*. The heart of the group is Mitsui & Co., the world's largest *sogo shosha* (general trading company), with some 900 subsidiaries and associated firms worldwide. Other key members of the Mitsui Group include Mitsui Mutual Life Insurance, Mitsui O.S.K. Lines, and Sakura Bank, which has announced plans to merge with rival Sumitomo Bank. Other Mitsui operations include chemicals, construction, logistics, mining, petroleum, real estate, textiles, and retailing.

The Mitsubishi Group's primary units are Mitsubishi Heavy Industries (Japan's number one maker of heavy machinery), the Bank of Tokyo–Mitsubishi, and Mitsubishi Corporation, which provides organizational oversight. Mitsubishi Group's more than forty companies make everything from steel and power plants to cameras, cars, chemicals, clothing, consumer electronics, and textiles.

The "members" of the *keiretsu* are connected in many ways. Often, the senior executives belong to a group that meets a number of times during the year to exchange opinions about the businesses in the industrial group and reinforce relational contracts. Suppliers of parts and services also belong to the *keiretsu* and meet to collect and disseminate information about one another and their relations to other group members (some might say like a club). In addition to sharing information, the members share management and own shares in one another.

Observers of Japanese corporate governance usually identify the following as key characteristics: (1) reciprocal and control-oriented share ownership and (2) relational contracting.

Reciprocal and Control-Oriented Share Ownership

In 1996, individuals (public shareholders) owned only 22 percent of the outstanding shares of common stock of Japanese companies, and this percentage had steadily declined from 70 percent in 1949. Instead, ownership is concentrated in the hands of what are called control-oriented shareholders.

As we noted, one of the key features of a *keiretsu* is member cross-ownership. Until recently, about 25 percent of the stock of *keiretsu* members was owned by other members. This "family" ownership is buttressed by considerable holdings of the stock of family members by companies that, while not part of the family, have very close ties to the *keiretsu*, including banks that have loaned money to the firms.

These owners are the control-oriented owners. Their primary concerns are their commercial relationships with the business firms in which they hold stock. Thus, their objective is maximizing the relationship values and the financial/economic performance of the *keiretsu* as a whole, not maximizing the market value of any one company.

This objective of protecting the *keiretsu* as an entity or family causes control ownership to be stable over time and protects individual firms from hostile takeovers. *Keiretsu* members will not vote their shares in favor of a takeover group simply because the group has offered a very high price for the target company. Instead, the members will protect the existing management of the company in order to protect relationships within the industrial group and to ensure continued sales to group members. Consequently, no effective arms-length corporate control market for monitoring and controlling managers has existed in Japan.

This absence of arms-length monitoring and control of management is exacerbated by the fact that the boards of Japanese firms consist entirely of the company managers. The board of a Japanese company consists of up to twenty-five people, typically men over fifty and most likely past employees of the company. Japanese boards have no outside directors and few women, academics, or minority representatives. Diversity is not an attribute of Japanese corporate governance. So, who monitors and controls company management?

Monitoring and controlling is done by the other control owners themselves. The term *selective intervention* is used to describe this process—control owners selectively intervene when a company faces financial or other problems.

If a company is in financial distress, the company's lead bank may intervene and take effective control of the company for the *keiretsu* as a whole. The bank, which is itself an equity holder in the company, may pay off the debts the firm owes to non-*keiretsu* banks or companies, with other *keiretsu* members sharing the loss. Along the way, the directors of the troubled company are augmented or replaced by directors of the bank and other group members—an outcome that would be virtually impossible in the United States, where such actions would cause the bank's loans to be declared equity capital and not recoverable in bankruptcy.

Selective intervention is also a mechanism for restructuring *keiretsu* members—but again this is done by executives and board members of the other companies. So, no really effective outside discipline exists, other than the eventual failure of the *keiretsu* itself or the intervention of the government.

Relational Contracting

The term *relational contracting* is best understood as an alternative to the written legal contracts used in the United States as a means of specifying what is to be done, by whom, and how. In a broader sense, the term covers the favored status that members of a *keiretsu* possess relative to nonmembers for business transactions.

Japan's automotive industry is a good example of relational contracting at work. Toyota, for example, will sign long-term supply agreements with parts suppliers within the Toyota group. However, these agreements are primarily indications of a joint willingness to work together over an extended period of time, including agreements to cooperate in business ventures. Unlike the situation in the United States, where such agreements would be much more detailed with respect to the rights and responsibilities of the signers, the Japanese signers rely on trust and mutual respect for enforcement, with the expectation being that disputes will not be settled through the legal system.

One of the ways in which this trust is established and maintained, or at least was in the past, is through the lifetime employment policies of Japanese firms. Contracts or agreements would be made "in principle" between the managers of firms (individuals), each of whom would expect the other to honor any implicit as well as explicit terms of the agreement and not seek to take advantage of the other party. Such arrangements work in part because each manager knows that he will be with the firm indefinitely, as will his counterpart at the other firm, and that dishonoring any terms of the agreement would have severe consequences in terms of the individual's reputation. Again, think of the arrangements as ones between members of an extended family, with all the consequences that follow from family disloyalty.

This relational contracting is reinforced through cross-ownership of shares within the *keiretsu* and through implicit agreements to buy goods, parts, and services from other members even if the price is higher than that available from nonmembers. Such practices obviously compromise the public shareholders' interests in the individual firm, but, from a family group perspective, such non-arms-length transactions merely reallocate profits within the group, leaving total group profits about the same. After all, the member who may be paying a higher-than-market price for one item may be receiving a higher-than-market price for what it sells to others.

Relational contracting, along with cross-ownership of shares, is a way of solving the problems associated with having parts suppliers make investments in the specific machinery and technologies needed to produce the parts and locate their production facilities where the automotive assemblers need them—a problem that American companies coped with through vertical integration. The essence of the problem is how to get a parts supplier to make investments in the machinery needed to supply parts to, say, Krafft Motor Company, and also to build the parts manufacturing facility near a Krafft assembly plant. Once the investment has been made and the plant has been built, what is to prevent Krafft from trying to lower the price it is willing to pay for the parts because the supplier, having made the investments, is in a very weak bargaining position? One answer would be cross-ownership of shares by Krafft in the parts supplier and relational contracting. Another answer would be to have Krafft buy the parts supplier and make it part of the company.

A CRITIQUE OF THE *KEIRETSU*

Until recently, the *keiretsu* was probably even more insulated from capital market discipline than German corporations. No arms-length corporate control market existed, and many transactions among firms were based on relationships rather than prices. But, for the system to have survived and Japan to have prospered under it in the post-World War II era, the system must have been solving a variety of problems associated with promoting economic growth and efficiency.

Advantages of the *Keiretsu*

Perhaps the most often cited advantage of the Japanese system is the development of long-term relationships that would not be possible in an arms-length market governance system. These relationships make it relatively easier for Japanese firms to restructure agreements in the event of financial difficulties or if outcomes are very different from those that were expected. For example, suppose the development costs incurred by a parts manufacturer for producing a new part for a new vehicle line turn out to be much higher than anticipated. The likelihood that the parts manufacturer will be able to renegotiate the original agreement and "share" the losses with the *keiretsu* buyer is much greater in Japan than in the United States, at least historically. Hence, a Japanese manufacturer was more likely to undertake the development project initially and make the necessary investment as the project unfolded without seeking prior contractual guarantees from the purchaser. Both parties would know that if something went wrong (or much better than expected), both would be obligated to share the unexpected consequences.

At the larger firms in Japan, this long-term relationship carried over to workers as well in the form of lifetime employment (this was not usually the case for small firms). Although Japanese workers do not have formal board representation as workers in Germany do, they are considered important stakeholders whose needs matter a great deal. When Nippon Steel planned to diversify into some nonsteel areas in which the company had no experience, it decided to retain steelworkers even though they were not needed. Workers came to expect these outcomes, and the result was a labor force that was committed to the company.

Disadvantages of the *Keiretsu*

The major criticism of the *keiretsu* from an economic growth and efficiency perspective seems to be that the system makes structural change difficult. Without market forces at work, companies tend to do what they always have done, and rather than shutting down negative NPV operations (restructuring), they keep them going so as to maintain the status quo. Critics of the system charge that these policies are reinforced by the government, which also wants to maintain high employment levels and reduce the political costs typically associated with structural changes.

It is impossible to quantify the benefits and costs of the Japanese *keiretsu*, just as it is impossible to do so for German universal banking or the American market governance system. Historical and cultural forces are as important as "scientific" economic efficiency factors, if not more important. But we can look at what is happening in Japan just as we did with Germany. What we find is a gradual erosion of the traditional *keiretsu* system—an erosion that arguably dates from the deregulation of Japanese financial markets (dubbed the Big Bang) and the country's banking crisis.

Japanese Reforms

In 1996, Japan's finance minister promised a "big bang" that would match the deregulation of London's financial system in 1986. The objective was to liberalize and internationalize Japan's financial industry. The proposed reforms included removal of restrictions that prevented banks, insurance companies, and investment houses from competing with one another. Financial reforms were to be coupled with reforms in other areas, including the way goods were distributed from producer to consumer and rules governing employment practices. The motivation for the reforms, according to many Japanese officials, was to make Japanese industries competitive in a global economy.

The Big Bang officially started on April 11, 1998, with the elimination of fixed brokerage commissions and the partial liberalization of foreign exchange dealings and cross-border capital transactions. Additional reforms were scheduled through 2001. Among these were giving individuals greater choice over where to place their money, such as mutual funds, thereby moving funds out of banks and into pension funds and other intermediaries that would be more attuned to the needs of public investors and less to the survival of the *keiretsu*.

This 1998 Big Bang coincided with a major banking crisis. Estimates of bad loans in the banking industry ran as high as a trillion dollars, or about one-fifth of total bank assets. Many analysts, especially Western analysts, attributed these bad loans to the clubby arrangements and relationship (non-arms-length) transacting within *keiretsu*, which were supported by the government. Instead of effectively monitoring management and stopping the flow of credit to failing firms within the group, the banks continued to pour money into them. The result, according to critics, was a set of bloated and inefficient industries, rising unemployment, and falling stock prices. These industries, protected by government restrictions on trade, were able to charge the Japanese prices that were far above world market prices, and any group member that tried to compete on price was ostracized. For example, the construction industry promised not to buy cement from firms that sold at prices below the cement industry association price. When one company tried to buy low-cost Korean cement, Japanese longshoremen refused to unload it.

As the banking crisis worsened and the Japanese economy continued to stagnate, what some might call seismic changes began to occur. In 1999, the French automotive company, Renault, acquired a 36.8 percent stake in Nissan, part of a *keiretsu* that was in a weak financial position. Along with the stake came an announcement that 21,000 jobs would be eliminated and five factories closed. Then, in November 1999, NTT, Japan's leading telecommunications operator, said that it would cut 21,000 jobs by March 2003. And reports in the press in March 2000 tell about Japanese companies selling the shares they hold in one another (cross-holdings) at a faster rate than ever. The industries in which the cross-holdings are falling the fastest are airlines, railways, steel, and banking—generally identified as the poorest-performing industries. So, relationships seem to be unraveling and arms-length transactions seem to be becoming more important as the deregulation of Japan's economy continues.

CONVERGENCE OR DIVERSITY?

Will corporate governance systems around the world converge to a single model, or will a diversity of systems continue to exist? And, if convergence is the answer, will it be the Anglo-American market system that dominates, or will it be some other system?

An informative context for evaluating these questions is that of the globalization of product and financial markets. By globalization, we mean the removal of barriers to capital and trade flows, so that national markets are open to all comers and domestic firms do not receive special legal treatment. In this world, firms compete on price and quality, with the winners being those firms that can offer the best quality at the lowest price. Even more important, perhaps, the winners are those firms than can quickly adjust to changing market conditions, innovate, and respond to technological change—let's call this dynamic competition. So, the underlying economic question is: Does a particular governance system give a competitive advantage to those firms that adopt it? If so, all firms would be likely to adopt that system in order to remain dynamically competitive and survive.

However, suppose that the differences we have identified among market, banking, and relationship-based systems don't really affect the firm's competitive position or cost of capital, but simply represent different ways of solving similar problems—the old adage about there being many ways to skin a cat. If this is the case, then diversity among systems is likely to remain, with the differences being driven by cultural, political, and philosophical differences rather than economic efficiency factors. Economists have a name for this process: path dependence.

Path dependence means that the governance systems we observe around the world reflect the unique legal, political, and cultural conditions in a given country at a given time. Legal systems that did not protect the individual investor led to concentrated ownership structures. Political concerns about concentration of wealth and size led to systems that looked to markets and public ownership of corporations to solve economic efficiency and growth problems. Once in place, these governance systems evolved into their current form, as did the country's other institutions. The result is simply a different constellation of rules, regulations, and institutions designed to solve the problem of organizing and monitoring the modern corporation.

We find the idea of path dependence appealing, especially because it is rooted in the political economy of a country and the country's culture and traditions. Still, the evidence does suggest that governance systems that require government protection from competition or that hinder the firm's ability to compete dynamically in world markets are likely to disappear. And, we are inclined to the view that a market-based governance system is better able to respond to the changing dynamics of the marketplace than a relationship-based system designed to protect the weakest members of its group. Only time will tell; after all, it was only a dozen years ago that many observers had declared the market-based system obsolete.

OECD PRINCIPLES OF CORPORATE GOVERNANCE

In May 1999, the Organization for Economic Cooperation and Development (OECD) put out a set of corporate governance standards developed in conjunction with national governments and international agencies such as the World Bank and the International Monetary Fund as well as the private sector. The principles are intended to assist governments in their efforts to evaluate and improve the legal, institutional, and regulatory framework for corporate governance in their countries, and to provide guidance and suggestions for stock exchanges, investors, corporations, and other parties that have a role in the process of developing good corporate governance.

The motivation behind the OECD initiative was partly its

recognition that the overall health of a country's economy, its prospects for economic growth, and its economic efficiency were directly related to the corporate governance issues we have addressed in this book. The OECD notes in its *OECD Principles of Corporate Governance* that:

> good corporate governance enables companies to access financing from a much larger pool of investors and that if countries are to reap the full benefits of the global capital market, and if they are to attract long-term "patient" capital, corporate governance arrangements must be credible and well understood across borders. Even if corporations do not rely primarily on foreign sources of capital, adherence to good corporate governance practices will help improve the confidence of domestic investors, may reduce the cost of capital, and ultimately induce more stable sources of financing.

The principles are divided into five areas: the rights of shareholders, the equitable treatment of shareholders, the role of stakeholders, disclosure and transparency, and the responsibilities of the board. You can get a full listing and explanation of these principles at *www.oecd.org*. The principles effectively summarize the issues and points we have made throughout this book.

NOTES

CHAPTER 1

1. Adolf A. Berle, Jr., and Gardiner C. Means, *The Modern Corporation and Private Property* (New York: Macmillan, 1933).

2. The remainder of this chapter draws heavily on Fred R. Kaen, Allen Kaufman, and Larry Zacharias, "American Political Values and Agency Theory," *Journal of Business Ethics* 7 (November 1988): 805–820.

3. Walter Lippman, *Drift and Mastery: An Attempt to Diagnose the Current Unrest* (New York: M. Kennerly, 1914).

4. See Louis D. Brandeis, *The Curse of Bigness: Miscellaneous Papers* ed. O. Fraenkel (New York: Viking Press, 1934) and T. Veblen, *The Theory of the Business Enterprise* (New York: Charles Scribner's Sons, 1904).

5. John Kenneth Galbraith, *The New Industrial State* (Boston: Houghton Mifflin, 1967).

6. Adolf A. Berle, Jr., and Gardiner C. Means, *The Modern Corporation and Private Property* (New York: Harcourt, Brace, & World, 1968), p. 10.

7. Robin Marris, "Galbraith, Solow and the Truth About Corporation," *The Public Interest* 9, 1968, pp. 37–46.

8. Robert H. Hayes and William J. Abernathy, "Managing Our Way to Decline," *Harvard Business Review*, July–August 1980, pp. 67–77.

9. Michael C. Jensen and William Meckling, "Theory of the Firm: Managerial Behavior, Agency Costs, and Ownership Structure," *Journal of Financial Economics*, October 1976, pp. 305–360.

CHAPTER 2

1. "How TIAA-CREF Works for Better Corporate Governance," *Participant*, May 1999, pp. 10–11.

2. Colleen A. Dunlavy, "Corporate Governance in Late 19th Century Europe and the U.S.: The Case of Shareholder Voting Rights," in *Comparative Corporate*

211

Governance: The State of the Art and Emerging Research, ed. Klaus Hopt et al. (Oxford: Clarendon Press, 1998), pp. 5–39.

3. Alexandra Harney, "Restructuring Hands Culture Shock to Japanese Workers," *Financial Times*, November 2, 1999, p. 4.

CHAPTER 3

1. Burton G. Malkiel, "Returns From Investing in Equity Mutual Funds 1971 to 1991," *Journal of Finance* 50 (June 1995): 571.

2. The widely acknowledged expert on IPOs is Jay Ritter. See his "The Costs of Going Public," *Journal of Financial Economics* 19 (1987): 269–282 and "The Long-Run Performance of Initial Public Offerings," *Journal of Finance* 46 (1991): 3–27.

3. V. L. Bernard and J. K. Thomas, "Post-Earnings Announcement Drift: Delayed Price Response of Risk Premium?" *Journal of Accounting Research* 27 (Supplement 1989): 1–36.

4. David Bailey, "Coke, P&G May Rethink Terms of Venture," Reuters, July 5, 2001.

5. Holman W. Jenkins, "The New Business Casual: Prison Stripes," *Wall Street Journal*, March 13, 2002, p. A19.

CHAPTER 5

1. J. Randall Woolridge, "Competitive Decline: Is a Myopic Stock Market to Blame?" *Journal of Applied Corporate Finance*, (Spring 1988), v. 1: 26–36.

2. Su H. Chan, John Kensinger, and John D. Martin, "The Market Rewards Promising R&D—And Punishes the Rest," *Journal of Applied Corporate Finance* 5 (Summer 1992): 59–66.

3. Quaker Oats Company, 1998 Annual Report.

CHAPTER 6

1. Betsey McKay and Joann S. Lubin, "Behind Coke's Massive Cuts: An Impatient Board," *Wall Street Journal*, January 27, 2000, p. B1.

2. Georgia-Pacific 2000 Annual Review, p. 41.

3. Matt Krantz, "Europe's SAP Puts Its Stock in U.S. Hands," *Investor's Business Daily*, August 3, 1998.

4. "Bethlehem Steel Gets Waivers of New Worth Requirement," Reuters, Yahoo Finance, July 3, 2001.

5. "Corporate Germany Reaping the Rewards of Risk-Taking," *Financial Times*, August 11, 1998, p. 20.

6. For a summary, see Mitchell Berlin, "For Better or for Worse: Three Lending Relationships," *Business Review: Federal Reserve Bank of Philadelphia*, November–December 1996, pp. 3–12.

7. Myron Slovin and John E. Young, "Bank Lending and Initial Public Offerings," *Journal of Banking and Finance*, (1990), v. 14: 729–740.

8. Diana Preece and Donald J. Mullineaux, "Monitoring, Loan Renegotiability and Firm Value: The Role of Lending Syndicates," *Journal of Banking and Finance*, (1996), v. 20: 577–594.

9. Ulrich Hartmann, from speech to the German-American Chamber of Commerce.

CHAPTER 7

1. Genuine Parts Corporation, 2000 Annual Report, p. 5.

2. Rafael La Porta, Florencil Lopez-De-Silanes, Andrei Shleifer, and Robert W. Vishny, "Agency Problems and Dividend Policies," *Journal of Finance* 55 (February 2000): 1–34.

3. Georgia-Pacific 2000 Annual Report, p. 41,

4. Genuine Parts Company 2000 Annual Report, p. 4.

CHAPTER 8

1. An excellent survey of the theoretical and empirical literature on executive compensation is Kevin Murphy, *Executive Compensation*, working paper, Marshall School of Business, University of Southern California, April 1998.

2. George W. Fenn and Nellie Liang, "Corporate Payout Policy and Managerial Stock Incentives," working paper 1999–23, *Finance and Discussion Series*, Board of Governors of the Federal Reserves System, 1999.

3. G. Bennett Stewart III, "EVA: Fact and Fantasy," *Journal of Applied Corporate Finance* 7 (Summer 1994): 71–84.

4. "The Boss's Pay," *Wall Street Journal*, April 12, 2001, p. R11.

5. Joann S. Lublin, "CEOs Pay Last Year Was Lowest Since 1989," *Wall Street Journal*, March 5, 2002, p. A6.

6. Carol Hymowitz, "Does Rank Have Too Much Privilege?" *Wall Street Journal*, February 26, 2002, p. B1.

CHAPTER 9

1. Steven Lipin, "When Managers Are the Buyers and the Sellers, Holders Beware," *Wall Street Journal*, October 5, 2000, p. C1.

CHAPTER 10

1. Michael E. Porter, "Capital Choices: Changing the Way America Invests in Industry," *Journal of Applied Corporate Finance* 5, no. 2 (Summer 1992): 4–16.

2. Peter L. Bernstein, "Are Financial Markets the Problem or the Solution? A Reply to Michael Porter," *Journal of Applied Corporate Finance* 5, no. 2 (Summer 1992): 17–22.

3. TIAA-CREF Policy Statement on Corporate Governance, TIAA-CREF, New York.

4. Melissa Hankins, "Battle Over the Boardroom," *Wall Street Journal*, April 12, 2001, p. R6.

5. "Tyco Paid Director for Advisement on CIT Merger," *Monitor Daily*, January 29, 2002, *www.monitordaily.com/story_page.cfm?News_id*.

6. Janet Elliott, "UT Dean's Enron Ties Questioned," *Houston Chronicle*, January 17, 2002, *www.HoustonChronicle.com*.

7. Ira M. Millstein and Paul W. MacAvoy, "The Active Board of Directors and Performance of the Large Publicly Traded Corporation," *Columbia Law Review* 98 (June 1998).

CHAPTER 11

1. "Pull Up the Drawbridge," *Economist*, July 7, 2001, p. 67.

2. William Boston and Paul Hofheinz, "Once Again, EU Takes a Back Seat to VW," *Wall Street Journal*, February 27, 2002, p. A16.

3. "Repackaged Hoechst Will Let Market Decide," *Financial Times*, November 7, 1996, p. 33.

4. Ulrich Hartmann, VEBA AG 1997 Shareholders' Meeting. May 22, 1997.

5. Matt Krantz, "Europe's SAP Puts Its Stock in U.S. Hands," *Investor's Business Daily*, August 3, 1998.

INDEX

About the Author

Fred R. Kaen is Professor of Finance and Co-Director of the International Private Enterprise Center at the Whittemore School of Business and Economics of the University of New Hampshire. He teaches courses in corporate finance, corporate governance, and international financial management. His research focuses on international finance, corporate governance and corporate finance and has been published in many leading academic journals. Professor Kaen has held visiting positions at the University of Oregon, The Norwegian School of Economics and Business (Bergen), the Norwegian School of Management (Oslo), the University of Hamburg, and the Budapest University of Economic Sciences and Admininstration.